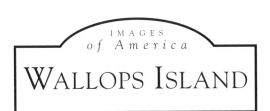

IMAGES
of America

WALLOPS ISLAND

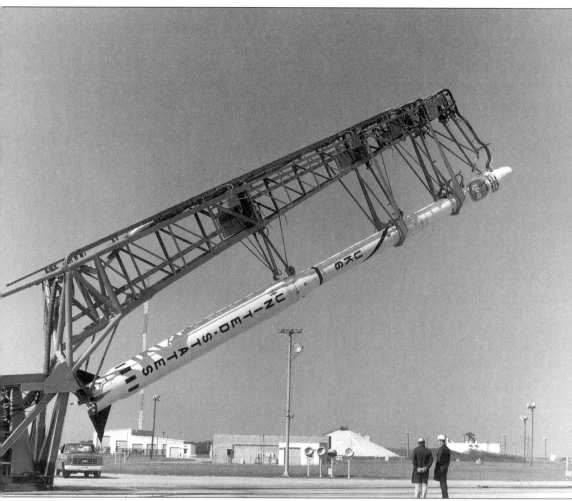

U-K 6. This Scout launch vehicle will launch a British Satellite U-K 6, which conducts scientific studies in the field of high-energy astrophysics. The satellite weighs 340 pounds and once in orbit will become Ariel 6. The satellite is designed to last for two years and will provide information regarding radio galaxies, supernovae, and pulsars, among other things. The U-K 6 program was conducted on a cost reimbursable basis between the United Kingdom's Science Research Council and NASA. The British flag and the Scout emblem denote that this is the 100th Scout launch. (Photo courtesy of NASA and the Wallops Flight Facility.)

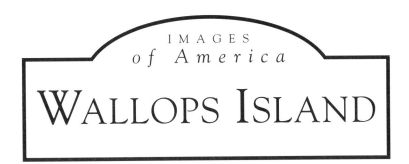

IMAGES
of America

WALLOPS ISLAND

Nan DeVincent-Hayes and Bo Bennett

ARCADIA

Published by Arcadia Publishing,
an imprint of Tempus Publishing, Inc.
2 Cumberland Street
Charleston, SC 29401

Printed in Great Britain.

Library of Congress Catalog Card Number: 00-110540

For all general information contact Arcadia Publishing at:
Telephone 843-853-2070
Fax 843-853-0044
E-Mail sales@arcadiapublishing.com

For customer service and orders:
Toll-Free 1-888-313-2665

Visit us on the internet at http://www.arcadiapublishing.com

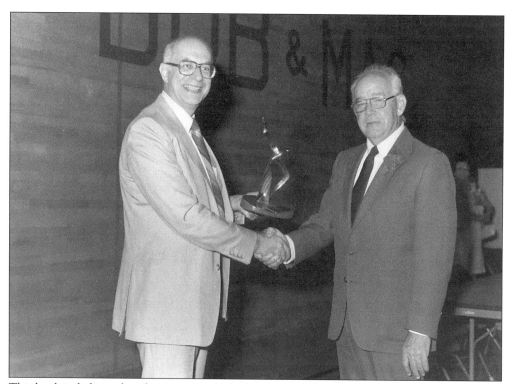

This book is dedicated to the memory of Abraham Spinak (1925–1997), associate director, and Richard L. Krieger (1930–1990), director of Wallops Island, who dedicated the major part of their lives to further the world's knowledge of space and flight science at Wallops Flight Facility.

CONTENTS

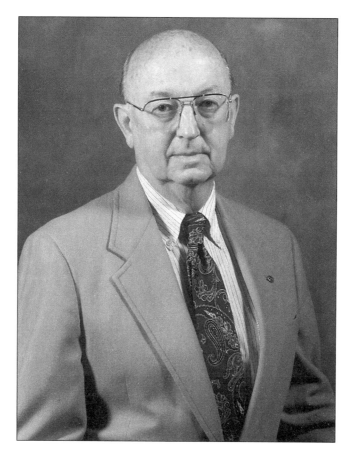

Since 1945, research activities at Wallops Flight Facility (WFF) have made significant contributions to the national aerospace program. WFF has produced cutting-edge scientific and technological advances, from the first National Advisory Committee for Aeronautics (NACA) rocket-propelled test vehicles that conducted aerodynamic research through the speed of sound and into the supersonic range of speeds and continuing on to include a broad array of National Aeronautics and Space Administration (NASA) programs.

In recent years, rockets, large balloons, and aircraft have been developed as launchers with appropriate platforms for scientific exploration, satellite instrument development, collaborating scientific measurements, and advanced technology development. These capabilities are used worldwide. WFF is presently recognized as the center of suborbital programs with agency project management responsibility for the Sounding Rocket and Scientific Balloons Programs. The test range now includes a research airport. The tracking and data acquisition capabilities developed to support all of these programs has been expanded to support satellites in orbit.

Facilities and services have been developed with a desire to attain a flexibility and responsiveness to continually varying requirements. An espirit de corps, instilled by longtime director Robert L. Krieger, permeates Wallops Flight Facility staff, ensuring high levels of success and producing an ideal work environment.

I personally consider it an honor and a privilege to be associated with Wallops Flight Facility.

—Robert T. Duffy

INTRODUCTION

Having visited the town of Chincoteague, Virginia, enough times to pen a book on it, we found ourselves forever facing Wallops Island, since one has to ride through the perimeter of the complex to get to Chincoteague and Assateague. It was then that we realized the value of this NASA-Goddard complex and determined that it should be given pages on which its own story might be told. Thus began a long siege of investigation, visits, pure research, endless phone calls, countless interviews, and unending questions. Through the untiring help of public relations officer Keith Kohler and his assistant, Betty Flowers, as well as interviews with the Krieger and Spinak families (along with the use of all their papers and pictures), we were able to piece together a pictorial history of the major developments and achievements of NASA's Wallops Island Facility from the time of its inception to the present.

NASA's Wallops Island Flight Facility, located in Accomac County, Virginia, on the Atlantic coast of the Delmarva (Delaware, Maryland, Virginia) Peninsula, is made up of three parts: Wallops Main Base, Wallops Mainland, and Wallops Island. Other than Salisbury, Maryland, about 45 miles away, the hub of the Eastern Shore and the closest town to Wallops is Chincoteague, Virginia, with about 3,200 residents. Over the years, Wallops has gone through numerous transformations—from mission conversions to name changes. From 1945 to 1947, Wallops was referred to as the Pilotless Aircraft Research Station (PARS), where high-speed rocket models were launched; from 1958 to 1974, it was called Wallops Station, which came under NASA and its Civilian Space Program. Another change occurred in 1975 and lasted through 1981 when the station was called Wallops Flight Center and added to its mission the study of ocean processes. Lastly, in 1982, the base merged with Goddard and became known as the Wallops Island Goddard Space Flight Center, which serves as a primary NASA research center to this day.

What a complex history Wallops Island has had. With step-by-step and stage-by-stage incremental footprints—both failures and successes—the island helped to lead America to the forefront in the space race. We learned that before rockets could be designed and built to launch space capsules that basic obstacles first had to be overcome, such as aerodynamic drag, heat transfer, wing stability and flutter, nose cone design, and many other factors. Most people mistakenly think that scientists just sit down and sketch out the type of rocket that will be built, when in reality before an entire vehicle can even be blueprinted, its constraints must first be dealt with and conquered. This is a long and time-consuming, as well as expensive, process. Each small hurdle had to be surmounted in order to confront and triumph over the bigger ones. This often meant creating scaled down models of proposed finished products, such as rockets, that must work perfectly in test flights. Many times this required taking the prototype back to the lab and redesigning and rebuilding it and then testing it again, only to repeat the process over and over until the scientists got it right. Other times it meant entirely aborting a project simply because if it couldn't be made to work in its archetype form, it wouldn't work in its full scaled version. Failures, which are usually the norm in creating a product from scratch, meant going back to the drawing board and re-designing the failed part or parts, and again testing it. It is incredible that the early WWF personnel had the determination, patience, persistence, dedication, and faith to take the many baby steps that eventually resulted in huge strides in the space race.

What you will see in this book is a simplified presentation of a very complicated process. Since we are not rocket scientists (excuse the pun) attempting to write a text book on aeronautical techniques, we figure you are not rocket scientists wanting to learn every system in aerospace studies. So what we've done in this history is to entertain you while providing a sense of how WFF came into existence, grew, served as a leader in the space race to bring us where we are today, and what its goals are for tomorrow. In this work, we allow you to take those same baby steps through history that have led to an upright posture of a futuristic millennium.

We hope you'll find the enclosed as pleasing as we have found it complex, and that perhaps it will awaken a sense of pride in you for your country as well as an appreciation for those who struggled so hard to make America a leader instead of a follower. Most of all, we hope that you will enjoy the book, and allow yourself to step back into history, travel to the present, and hazard a leap to the future.

Nan DeVincent-Hayes, Ph.D
Bo Bennett, B.A.

ACKNOWLEDGMENTS

We would like to thank Keith Kohler and Betty Flowers of the Public Relations Department at Wallops Island for their patience and hospitality in answering endless questions and supplying us with photographs for this project. A warm thank you to the families of Robert L. Krieger and Abe Spinak, who were immense helps. Our gratitude also goes to those of you who gave of your time for interviews: Emmett Taylor, John Hall, Jack Clark, Timmy McCready, Dave Kulley, Vernon McIntyre, Bobby Lappin, Phillip Daffin, Richard E. Jenkins, Lynn Krieger Hines, Jack Krieger, Robert Krieger, Karen Krieger, Ruth Spinak, Barry Spinak, Dennis Rajala, Janice Wallop and family, Jill Jester, Orland Howard, Ronnie Rodgers, Lt. Commander Mark Ogle, Robert Duffy, and Bob Jacobs, as well as to all those of you who we may have omitted in this acknowledgment. We are also grateful for the use of the books by Joseph Adams Shortal and Harold D. Wallace Jr. and Curtis Badger. A special thanks to Bo's fiance, Johnny C. Townsend, for his numerous errands and assistance in creating this book; to Nan's husband, Jim Hayes, for his endless help with the computer and formatting of the book, as well as assistance in typing; to Nan's daughters Brynnne and Marta Hayes, and Bo's son Stephen, for their continued understanding of the demanding hours taken away from them while working on this book. Also a special nod goes to our friends and family, who have been understanding about our limited time spent with them. To all of you, we offer our heartfelt thanks.

One
HISTORY OVERVIEW

Wallops Island Flight Facility (WFF) has a rich and vivid history, starting with its early days when it was no more than a primitive terra firma sporting overgrowth, one or two decrepit buildings, and hordes of mosquitos. Civilization was unheard of, and yet, this very antediluvian expanse would become home not only to some of the world's brightest scientists but also a center of sophisticated technology that would one day serve as the originator, progenitor, and prototype for putting men on the moon. From its early years as a flight test facility to its present days as a contender for serving as home to Venture Star, WFF has been the drive behind the development of rockets and launchers, as well as space research, that brought about the likes of the Atlas, the Scout, Mercury, Challenger, and a slew of other space ships that would not be in existence today if it hadn't been for the Wallops base and the workers who persisted and persevered in finding ways to overcome the problems of space flight.

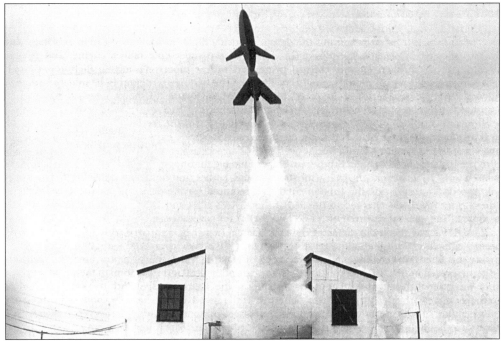

TIAMATS. The Tiamat missiles were the first type of rocket to be launched for Langley from WFF. Although officially titled the MX-570, the Tiamat was an air-to-air missile. This particular project set the tone and pace for the Wallops base because, up until this point, a number of obstacles had to be overcome before the first missile could be developed and launched. (Courtesy of Joseph Adams Shortal.)

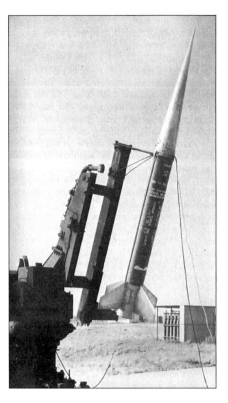

HEAT TRANSFER. Between 1945 and 1957, when WFF was under NACA's reign, the base focused on researching the effects of high temperatures on rockets as they sped through the air. Without overcoming the resistance of heat, rockets couldn't be launched, and transonic and supersonic flights could not have come to fruition. Likewise, if supersonic speed wasn't attainable because of the heat transfer problem, then the goal of bringing about sub-orbiting and orbiting piloted capsules would never have come about, leaving America behind in the space race. The diligent engineers at WFF conquered the problem, and we have since bypassed the goals of piloted orbits. (Courtesy of Joseph Adams Shortal.)

A WEATHER BALLOON. Although the goal of WFF has always been to put humans into space via the development of capsules and through serving as a test base, WFF did shift its emphasis to developing sounding rockets and the creation and testing of weather balloons, though even today it remains the principle facility for testing and managing the implementation of suborbital research programs. Besides sounding rockets and balloon programs, SELVS (Small Expandable Launch Vehicles) launch support earth science studies are also chief concerns of Wallops Flight Facility, along with providing flight services for scientific investigations. WFF also operates a test range and orbital tracking station. In this photo we see a scientific balloon prior to its launch. Compare its size to the figures at ground level. (Courtesy of Joseph Adams Shortal.)

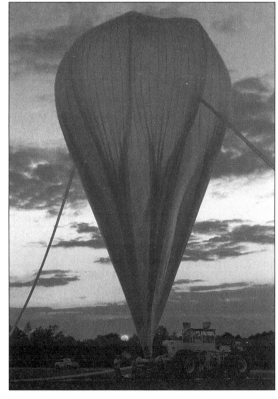

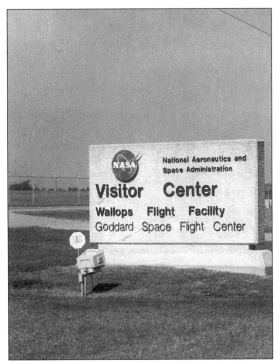

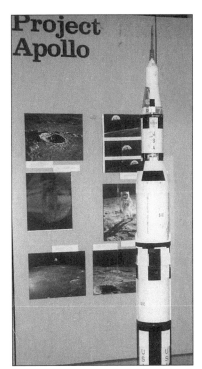

THE VISITOR CENTER. This collage of the Visitor Center gives only a sense of what's offered. The center can't be missed as you drive on Route 175 toward Chincoteague and Assateague, because you pass it on your right and are immediately struck by its rockets erected on launchers in the vertical position, pointing toward the heavens as though they were ready to ignite at a second's notice. The center contains a movie theater, racks of literature, and an outstanding museum that walks you through the development of the space age from its beginning at WFF to its present day symbols of *Challenger*, *Columbus*, and *Endeavor*, along with its strives for a global space station and the acquisition of Venture Star. From a small, primitive research base, WFF has taken its place as a behemoth in aeronautical research. *ABOVE, LEFT*: The Visitor Center's sign. *ABOVE, RIGHT*: The Apollo project, of which other bases are credited for its development, though WFF served as the leader in its design and creation. *BELOW*: The X-15 made for the Air Force as it's displayed in the museum. Notice its size and streamlined shape. (Photos by Bo Bennett.)

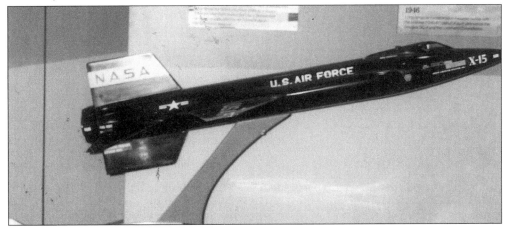

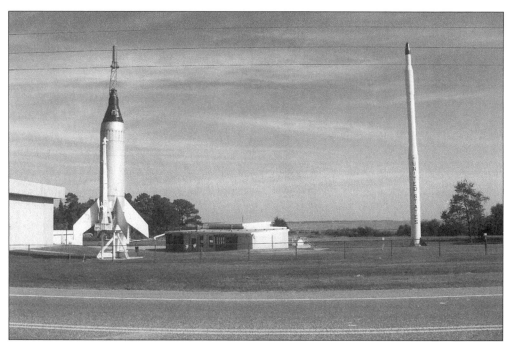

VISITOR CENTER ROCKETS. This is a sampling of the type of rockets one passes en route to Chincoteague. Spectators pull into the visitor's parking lot of WFF to watch various launches—all of which are open to the public and regularly scheduled on a flight agenda that is online at www.nasa.gov. Not only are these launches free, but they're heart-thrilling, educational, and awesome to watch. This is one part of the massive base where visitors are allowed to roam unrestricted. All other parts require clearance, registration, and badges for admission to non-classified areas. (Photo courtesy of Bo Bennett.)

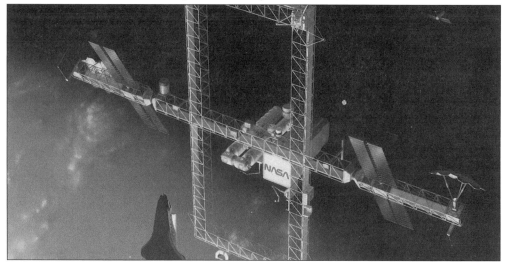

THE SPACE LAB. When we look at the sophisticated rockets of today zooming off to the moon or Mars, or when we listen to the reports of the world cooperative International Space Lab, we should remember that it all started at WFF from those small steps of research turning into giant steps of success. This image gives a feel of the advanced and wondrous space lab, which is still in existence today. (Courtesy of the Education Center.)

Robert L. Krieger
EDUCATION COMPLEX

———●———

DEDICATED IN HONOR OF

Dr. Robert L. Krieger
1916 – 1990

THE EDUCATION CENTER. Wallops Flight Facility is a beehive of activity within its secured grounds, but the complex has always served the general public as well as the government. Numerous educational programs have been implemented, including those originated by Robert Krieger. An education center exists for teachers and others needing resources on space studies, from small pamphlets to thick books—all free. Additionally, Wallops Flight Facility works in conjunction with various academic consortia as well as providing aeronautical programs at several universities. Internships are also available for high school and college studies. (Courtesy of the Robert L. Krieger family.)

MISSION 2000 STATEMENT. As WFF enters a new millennium, it is once again shifting to pursue programs that will better address America's and the world's needs and desires to form and share in a global space program. Sounding rockets, balloon studies, orbital tracking, management of scientific aircraft, earth science, shuttle payloads, and the maintenance of its launch range take a front and center role in the new era. The promising future for WFF has just begun. (Photo courtesy of Nasa Wallops Flight Facility Web Page.)

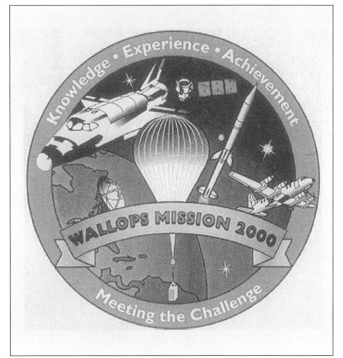

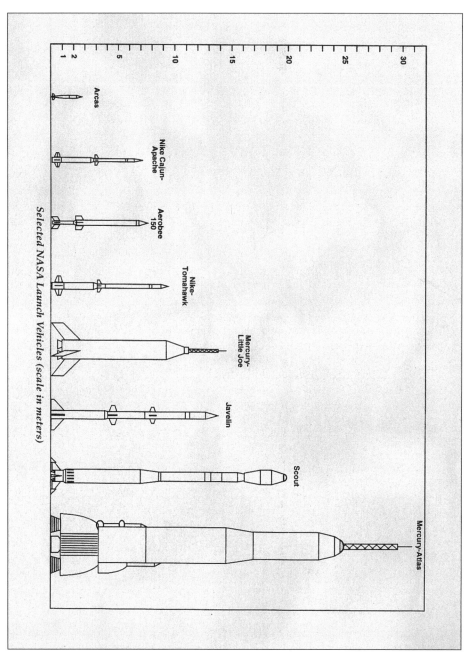

NASA Launch Vehicles. Wallops Island's engineers have been instrumental in testing all the original rockets that led to those breaking the sound barrier; sub-orbiting and then orbiting the earth; and, through NASA's other bases, going beyond Earth's atmosphere, touching down on the Moon and Mars, and setting up an international space lab. As a result, it is only fitting that we take a look at selected NASA scaled launch vehicles, depicted here in meters. The first is the *Arcas* at only about 2.5 meters compared to the scaled model of the Mercury-Atlas at over 35 meters. Note, too, Wallops' famous Nike models, their Little Joe, and, of course, the Scout. (Photo courtesy of Harold D. Wallace Jr.)

Two

JOHN WALLOP AND THE HUNT CLUB

John Wallop, a self-made millionaire and entrepreneur by today's standards, mapped most of Virginia's Eastern Shore three centuries ago, owning outright 2,385 acres himself. In the beginning of the 19th century, the present U.S. Route 13 from the Maryland state line to Zion Church Road, a distance of about 75 miles, was known as "Wallop's Road." This industrious man was a civic leader, surveyor, real estate purchaser, farmer, engineer, blacksmith, mariner, weaver, tanner, surgeon, and perhaps even a chemist.

In the 1600s Virginia had the status of a Crown Colony. The government decided to give to any immigrant who could get themselves over to the Virginia colony 50 acres of land. With numerous ways in which to obtain land, a person with any type of skill had the opportunity to own vast tracts of land.

John Wallop took advantage of these opportunities to amass large quantities of property. Being a mariner, he was able to obtain some of this acreage by transporting folks over to the new colony. An entry in the records of Accomack County shows a John Wallop acquiring 800 acres in head rights for transporting 16 passengers to the new colony.

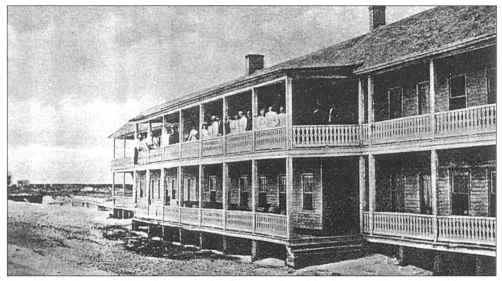

THE HUNT CLUB. In 1889 the entire island was purchased for the use of Pennsylvania hunters, who erected a clubhouse on the north end of the island. In 1945 this land was sold to NASA for Wallop's Station. (Photo courtesy of Barnes and Truitt.)

JOHN WALLOP

1641 – 1693

SURVEYOR – MARINER – EARLY SETTLER – CIVIC LEADER

ORIGINAL LAND PATENTEE OF:

WALLOPS STATION

"--- my two thousand three hundred and eight five acres of land at Gingoteague one the maine land of Accomack County ---"

WALLOPS ISLAND

"--- my Island formermorly called Keeckotank Island scituate on the Seaboard Side in Accomack County ---"

John Wallop was born about 1641, his place of birth and ancestory being unknown. By 1663 he was in Accomack County receiving a commision as a surveyor. From that year until 1693, the year of his death, he appears in the Accomack record every year.

During the the first few years he claimed many head rights and secured a number of patents. His first patent on Wallops Neck (Wallops Station) being in 1664. By 1666 he had completed the acquisition of the entire Neck. His first patent on Wallops Island was in 1672. Although Wallop was granted many other patents, totaling more than 6500 acres, his Wallops Neck and Wallops Island property seem to have been his main interest. By the time of his death he had disposed of all other real estate.

JOHN WALLOP. This scroll was created by Robert L. Krieger summarizing John Wallop's life as a surveyor, mariner, settler, and leader. Wallop held a total of 2,385 acres; by the time of his death in 1693 his land had been subdivided many times by the transfer of property from generation to generation. (Courtesy of the Krieger family.)

PONIES. Wild ponies were, for many years, the only inhabitants of the island. One favorite local legend of how the ponies came to occupy the island is that they survived a Spanish shipwreck in the 1800s. These hardy ponies swam ashore and lived on salt grass, poison ivy, and shrubbery. In 1945, when NACA purchased the island, it was decided that in the summer of 1946 the ponies would be rounded up and moved to Assateague Island. The men hoped that this would decrease the horsefly population and would also allow NACA to spray DDT for any remaining horseflies and pesky mosquitos without harming the animals. (Courtesy of Robert Stout.)

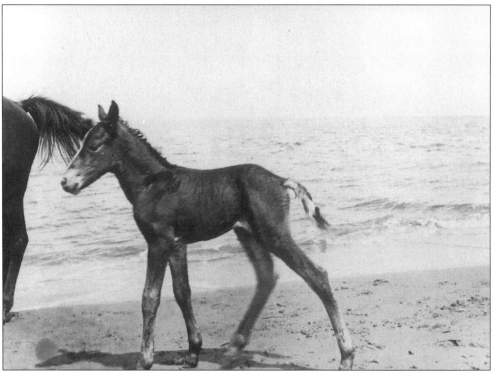

WALLOPS TODAY. Pictured here are Ned and Mary Jane Wallop. Over the years the island was divided among John Wallop's descendants, which Richard Krieger traced to its twelfth generation. Krieger also traced the division of property through the sixth generation. These parcels were eventually sold to outsiders. (Photo courtesy of Janice Wallop.)

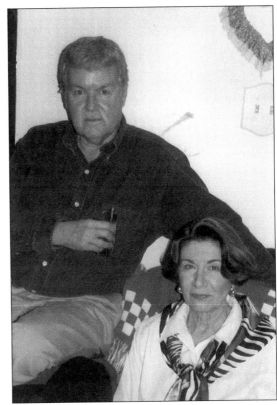

THE WALLOP FAMILY. This 1995 photograph represents the latest generation of Wallops who currently reside in Maryland. Pictured here are Jeff Wallop (standing behind the couch), and, from left to right on the couch, Janice, Chris, Mary Jane, and Tyler Wallop. The baby is Casey Wallop. (Photo courtesy of Janice Wallop.)

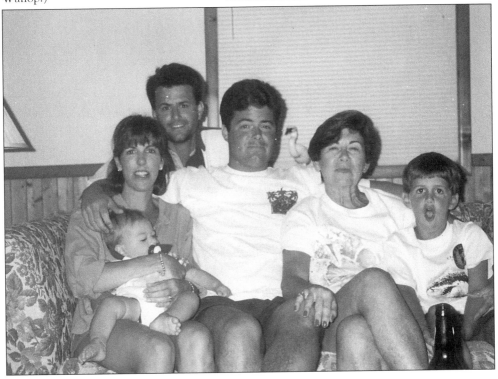

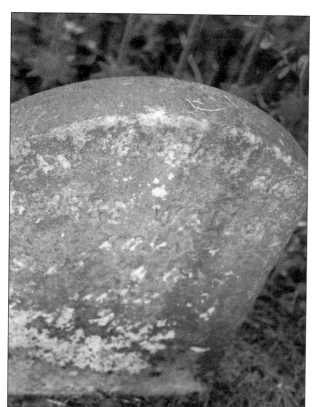

GEORGE WALLOP'S GRAVE.
George was in the sixth generation of the Wallop family. His grave is located south of the Maryland/Virginia state line in a graveyard on top of a little knoll behind a convenience store. The grave is the only one surrounded by a fence, as seen in the photograph below. At left is a close-up photograph of his actual gravestone, which is now barely legible. Richard Krieger visited his grave in the early 1960s and was able to discern the epitaph, which at time read "In memory of George Wallop, born September 26, 1818, Died April 2, 1888, Aged 69 years, 7 months, and 6 days, At Rest." George was born a year before the death of his father, John Wallop. The smaller gravestone in the forefront (below) is not mentioned by Krieger and may be a Wallop descendant. (Photo by Bo Bennett.)

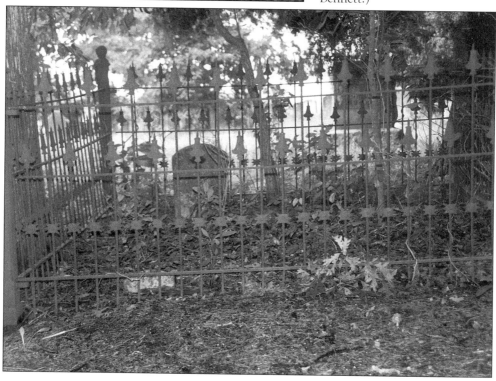

A GENEALOGY AND MAP OF THE PROPERTY. This chart depicts the genealogy of seven generations of John Wallops and his family as well as the division of property from generation to generation. The acreage is written with an "A" next to it and the year of the transaction is written underneath the acreage. Krieger writes "Altho John Wallop's will left a total of 2,385 acres to Skinner(2) and Sarah, the Survey of 1793 showed 2,450 acres. Deducting the 200 acres held by Dolby and the 300 acres held by Kendall shows that we should correct Skinner(4) holdings as shown." (Courtesy of the Krieger family.)

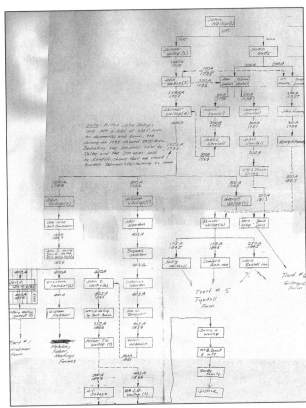

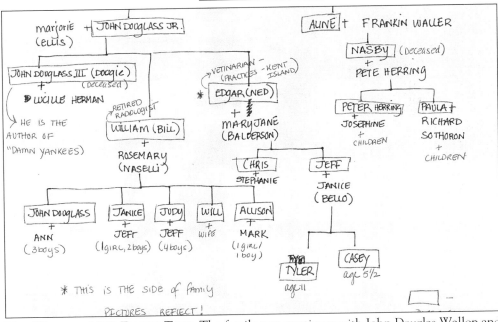

THE WALLOPS 2000 FAMILY TREE. The family tree continues with John Douglas Wallop and Berta Wallop being the ninth generation of Wallop families in this drawing that follows through to the twelfth generation. It is interesting to note that John Douglass "Doogie" Wallop III (eleventh generation) was the author of *Damn Yankees*. (Courtesy of Janice Wallop.)

19

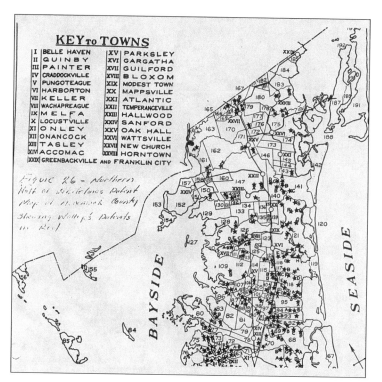

KEY TO TOWNS

I	BELLE HAVEN	XV	PARKSLEY
II	QUINBY	XVI	GARGATHA
III	PAINTER	XVII	GUILFORD
IV	CRADDOCKVILLE	XVIII	BLOXOM
V	PUNGOTEAGUE	XIX	MODEST TOWN
VI	HARBORTON	XX	MAPPSVILLE
VII	KELLER	XXI	ATLANTIC
VIII	WACHAPREAGUE	XXII	TEMPERANCEVILLE
IX	MELFA	XXIII	HALLWOOD
X	LOCUSTVILLE	XXIV	SANFORD
XI	ONLEY	XXV	OAK HALL
XII	ONANCOCK	XXVI	WATTSVILLE
XIII	TASLEY	XXVII	NEW CHURCH
XIV	ACCOMAC	XXVIII	HORNTOWN
XXIX	GREENBACKVILLE AND FRANKLIN CITY		

Figure 26 – Northern Half of Whitelaw's Patent Map of Accomack County Showing Wallop's Patents in Red

KEY TO TOWNS. Wallop's land is indicated by the stars on this map. According to Krieger, this is the "Northern half of Whitelaw's Patent Map of Accomack County showing Wallop's patents in real." (Courtesy of Whitelaw, Krieger and the Eastern Shore of Virginia Historical Society.)

Table I. John Wallop's Real Estate Transactions

Acquisitions				Sold			
Year	Location	From	Acres	Year	Location	Buyer	Acres
1664	A-166	Patent	400	1667	A-166	Frances Beston	600
1664	A-175	Patent	1000	1668	A-132	Wm Walthom	300
1666	A-166	Patent	400	1669	A-166	Wm Beston	200
1666	A-132	Patent	300	1669	A-175	John Micheal	700
1666	A-175	Patent	700	1672	A-176	Thomas Mayson	650
1666	A-175	Wm Waters	1350	1676	A-182	Jock Tarr	225
1668	A-174	Som Taylor	35	1677	A-182	Jonathon Owen	225
1672	A-182	Patent	100				
1672	A-196	Patent	650				
1672	A-142	Patent	1450				
1674	A-182	Patent	350				
1692	A-142	Patent	50				
Total			6785				2900
			2900				
Total Retained			3885				

JOHN WALLOP'S REAL ESTATE TRANSACTIONS. This key depicts the patents that Wallop obtained between 1664 and 1692 and also shows the land that was sold between 1667 and 1677. Wallop did not start selling land until three years after his first patent. At that time he had a total of 4,150 acres. (Courtesy of the Krieger family.)

WALLOPS NECK, 1692. This map belonging to Richard Krieger shows the original 2,385 acres owned by John Wallop. Krieger traced the boundaries of land from his will. Wallop served as a deputy surveyor to Edmund Scarburg, who was the surveyor general in 1663. This enabled Wallop to add to his rapidly growing ownership of the Wallop's Island area. The land was originally used to graze cattle and horses. (Courtesy of the Krieger family.)

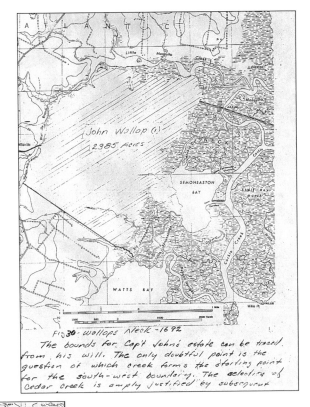

WALLOP'S LAND, FIFTH GENERATION, 1795. This map shows the difference in the acreage by the fifth generation. John Wallop (5) owned 1,200 acres and the rest was subdivided among William, George, and Henry Wallop. Skinner (4) was responsible for deeding more acreage than he actually owned to his three sons. (Courtesy of the Krieger family.)

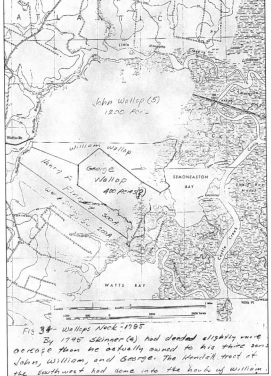

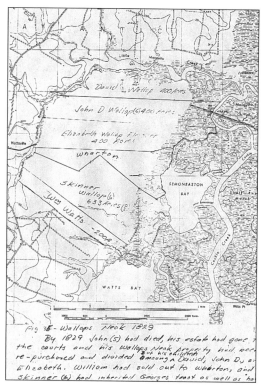

AN 1829 MAP OF WALLOP'S LAND. This map further illustrates the division of land among David, John, Elizabeth, and Skinner Wallop. Richard Krieger notes "By 1829 John (5) had died, his estate had gone through the courts and his Wallops neck property had been purchased and divided among his children David, John David, Elizabeth. William had sold out to Wharton, and Skinner (6) had inherited George's tract as well as having purchased Henry Finney's land . . ." (Courtesy of the Krieger family.)

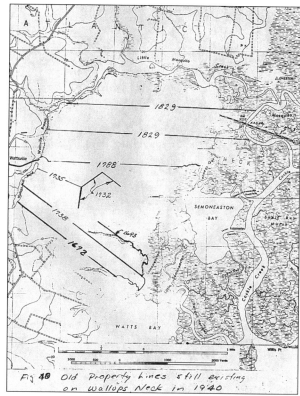

WALLOP'S LAND, 1900S. The property lines that still existed in 1940 are shown here on Wallops Neck. (Courtesy of the Krieger family.)

22

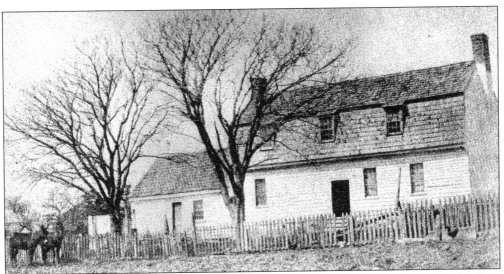

A WALLOP HOUSE. This home is believed to have once belonged to a member of the Wallops family. The structure is from the later part of the 18th century. It is known that Skinner Wallop died in 1718 and George Wallop lived from 1818 to 1888. It seems very possible that this may indeed be the a home of a Wallop. (Courtesy of Virginia Historical Society.)

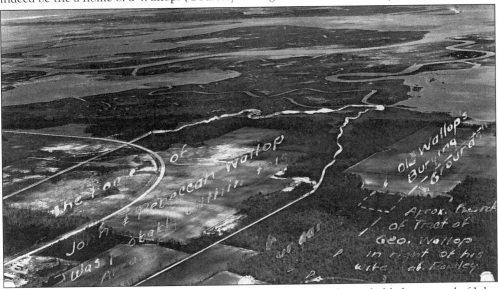

AN AERIAL VIEW OF WALLOP'S LAND. This aerial map shows the probable homestead of John and Rebecca Wallop. It also shows the old Wallop's burying ground, which Richard Krieger was able to find. Krieger located the cemetery in a wooded area. He estimated the surrounding trees to be at least 50 to 60 years old in 1960. He found one tree in particular that had a wide girth, and noted that this tree had grown through a fallen tree of equal girth—and so was probably at least 200 years old. Krieger suspected the graveyard was of the same age. David Wallop's (6) daughter Mary was buried here next to her mother. According to Krieger, her headstone read "Mary Douglas, consort of Edward K. Snead, and daughter of David and May Wallop. Born September 1880, Died November 8, 1869." These dates are incorrect; either the dates were transposed by Krieger or they may have been carved incorrectly on the gravestone itself. The traces of other old graves could not be discerned. (Courtesy of Richard L. Krieger's family.)

WALLOPS ISLAND ASSOCIATION
Names and Addresses of Members
October 1, 1927

1. Baker, J. E. York, Pa.
2. Beahm, R. B., 413 Lewis Building, Philadelphia, Pa.
3. Beecher, J. W. Pottsville, Pa.
4. Bye, Chas. C. Holly Oak, Del.
5. Crichton, Alex, F., c/o Union Nat. Bank Bldg., Wilmington, Del.
6. Elverson, Mrs. J. S., Catasauqua, Pa.
7. Emery, J. B. Williamsport, Pa.
8. Frame, Mrs. Florence Rick, Reading, Pa.
9. Fuller, J. W., Jr., Catasauqua, Pa.
10. Gilbert, P. J., York, Pa.
11. Hardt, Dr. Albert F., 414 Pine St., Williamsport, Pa.
12. Heilman, T. Newton, Williamsport, Pa.
13. Hoober, John A., York, Pa.
14. Hunter, P. Frank, Jr., Norristown, Pa.
15. Kegler, E. G., York, Pa.
16. Kerr, Chas. M., Wrightsville, Pa.
17. Lewis, S. S., York, Pa.
18. Markle, Alvan, Hazleton, Pa.
19. Otto, L. M., Jr., Williamsport, Pa.
20. Patterson, S. W., 1637 Fifth Ave.,Huntington, W.Va.
21. Shoemaker, Chas., 4917 N. 13th St., Philadelphia, Pa.
22. Ryder, F. P., 700 Liberty Bldg., Philadelphia, Pa.
23. Skelly, J. T., c/o Hercules Powder Co., Wilmington, Delaware.
24. Stout, F. W., Bethlehem, Pa.
25. Thaeler, Mrs. Ruth C. S., Nazareth, Pa.
26. Trexler, Harry C., Allentown, Pa.
27. Whiteley, Mrs. Purdon Smith, York, Pa.
28. Wilton, Fred M., Wrightsville, Pa.
29. Wilton, Ralph P., Wrightsville, Pa.
30. Woodbury, Wesley K., Pottsville, Pa.

MEMBERS OF THE WALLOP'S ISLAND ASSOCIATION. Wallops Island was owned by a group of Pennsylvania sportsmen in the early 1900s. The land was originally purchased for $8,000 by a Philadelphia gentlemen named Wesley K. Woodbury, acting for the "Wallops Land Association," whose name is on the end of this list. This hunting lodge/summer resort was operated until the start of World War II. It was sold in 1945 to NASA after a supplemental appropriation was passed by Congress to authorize expanded research on guided missiles at NACA Langley Laboratory, including the establishment of a rocket launch facility at Wallops Island. (Courtesy of Richard L. Krieger's family.)

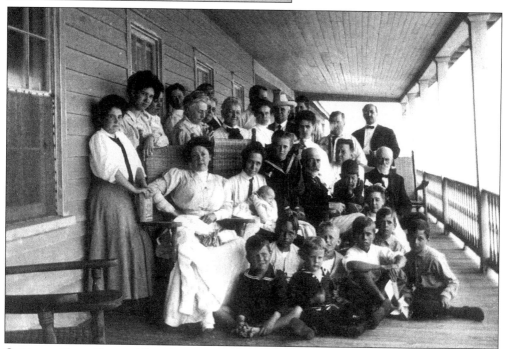

COUNTRY CLUB GROUP. This elite group of families traveled to Wallops Island from Delaware, Pennsylvania, and West Virginia to gather in the summer to enjoy life on the island. The families had a grand place to turn in after a day of swimming, fishing, and playing on the beach. (Courtesy of Richard L. Krieger's family.)

MINUTES. The 38th annual meeting of the Wallops Island Association was held in Pennsylvania at the Bellevue Stratford Hotel on October 16, 1928. Land on the island was leased to Joseph S. Pruitt to pasture his ponies and sheep. Additionally, Pruitt was given oyster and clam rights. However, there was a stipulation that required him to have a full-time watchman guarding his livestock and shellfish along with the property of the landowners. (Courtesy of Robert Stout and the Eastern Shore of Virginia Historical Society, Wallops Island Collection.)

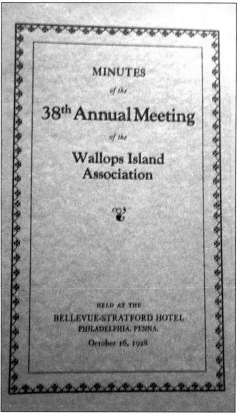

LOCAL CATCH. This Pennsylvania gentleman holds his catch of the day. In the 1920s a variety of fish were caught off the shore including, flounder, croaker, hogfish, bluefish, and butterfish. The gentleman on the left is smoking a cigar and wears a loose jacket over his clothes. All of the people are wearing bonnets or hats to protect them from the sun, since it was considered "lower class" to have a tan. (Courtesy of Robert Stout and the Eastern Shore of Virginia Historical Society, Wallops Island Collection.)

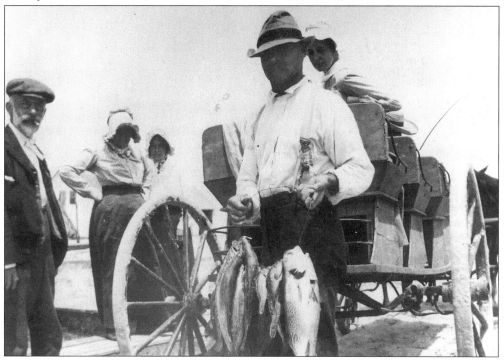

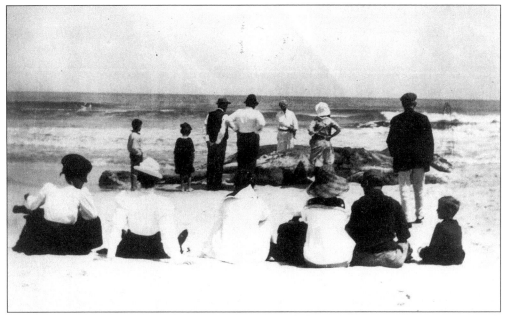

BEACHED WHALE. A variety of whales travel up and down the East Coast between South America and Canada; here, two whales lie dead surrounded by curious beachgoers. These whales may be pilot or humpback, which are common for this area. Whales intentionally beach themselves to die for a variety of reasons, be it biological (they have cancer) or environmental. A row of spectators sit and watch from a distance as the braver individuals go in for a closer look. (Courtesy of Robert Stout and the Eastern Shore of Virginia Historical Society, Wallops Island Collection.)

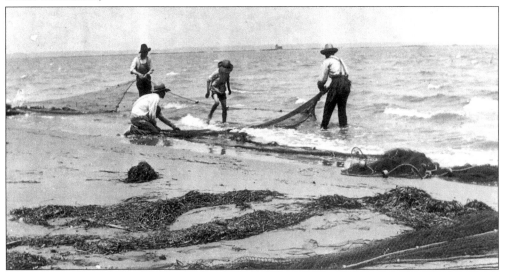

FISHING NETS ABOUND. These hardy fishermen have their work cut out for them. The wet nets are straightened and taken out in a straight line into the water with a boat at the other end. When enough fish swim into the net, the boat will swing around and bring the net back onto itself. The resulting catches were usually quite handsome, with up to hundreds of fish in one day. (Courtesy of Robert Stout and the Eastern Shore of Virginia Historical Society, Wallops Island Collection.)

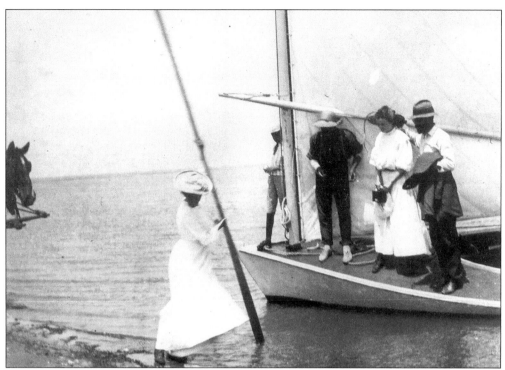

PRECARIOUS JUMP. The horse partly visible in the upper left-hand corner of the photograph probably indicates that there is a three-seated buggy waiting for these passengers to disembark from the boat. A women balances herself on the pole using it in a similar fashion as a pole vaulter would, to get from the boat to the shore without getting her skirt wet. (Courtesy of Robert Stout and the Eastern Shore of Virginia Historical Society, Wallops Island Collection.)

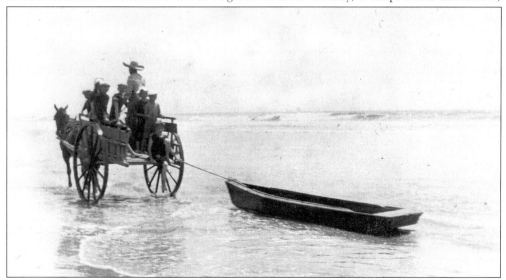

PULLING BOAT. A horse-drawn cart is pulling a boat to a different location down the beach. This early 1900s version of a trailer includes many children that keep the driver company as they make their way to their next destination. (Courtesy of Robert Stout and the Eastern Shore of Virginia Historical Society, Wallops Island Collection.)

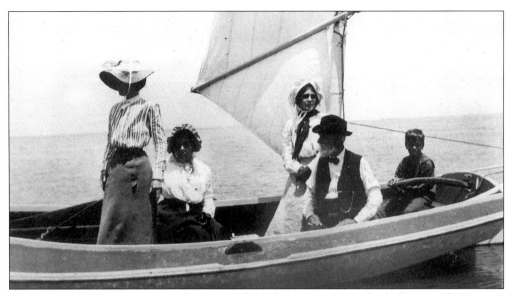

SAILBOAT. Vacationers take a ride on a sailboat known as a seaside skiff. These boats were popular on the Eastern Shore because their shape allowed them to maneuver easily in the shallow water. They could be used for fishing or transportation. The boy in the back is apparently the skipper of the boat. Everyone is wearing long sleeves—one wonders how people wore such stifling clothes in the summer. The gentlemen has a pocket watch, which was fashionable for the time period and is indicative of his upper-class status. (Courtesy of Robert Stout and the Eastern Shore of Virginia Historical Society, Wallops Island Collection.)

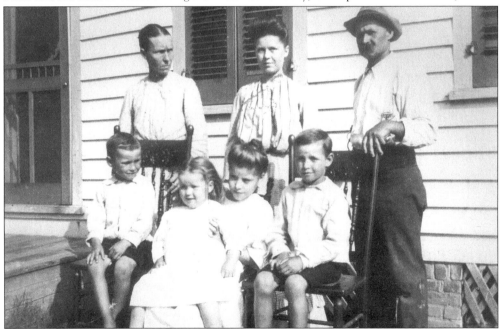

FAMILY PHOTO. This family gathers for a photo outside their home. Interestingly, the woman on the left is glaring at the man on her left, who is scowling. Fortunately, the rest of the family seems to be in a fine mood on this sunny summer day. (Courtesy of Robert Stout and the Eastern Shore of Virginia Historical Society, Wallops Island Collection.)

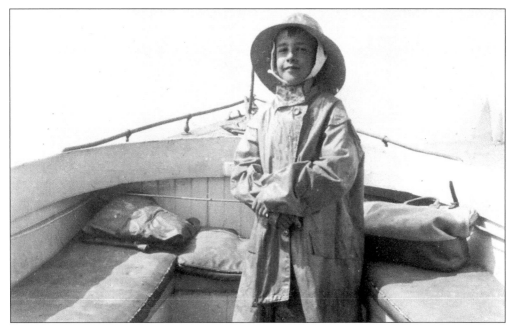

SKIPPER. This boy is bundled up in oversized foul weather gear ready to ride across the bay. The carpet and seats on the vessel suggest this boat was used to transport passengers to and from the island. (Courtesy of Robert Stout and the Eastern Shore of Virginia Historical Society, Wallops Island Collection.)

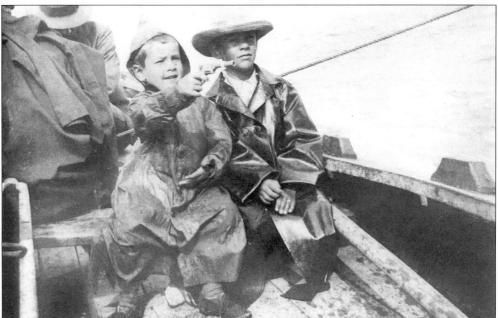

TOY GUN. The little boy on the left points his toy gun as this photographer snaps his photo. The wooden plank the boys are seated on in the stern of the boat looks crowded with a sail that a man in the back of the photo is working on. Their oversized rain jackets are repelling the sea spray off of them as well as keeping them warm. (Courtesy of Robert Stout and the Eastern Shore of Virginia Historical Society, Wallops Island Collection.)

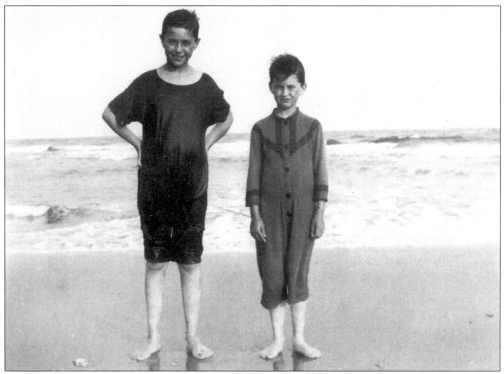

BOYS GOING FOR A SWIM. These boys look comfortable enough in their suits, which are made of wool. Typical suits were knee length or just below and came in long or short sleeves, as shown here. (Courtesy of Robert Stout and the Eastern Shore of Virginia Historical Society, Wallops Island Collection.)

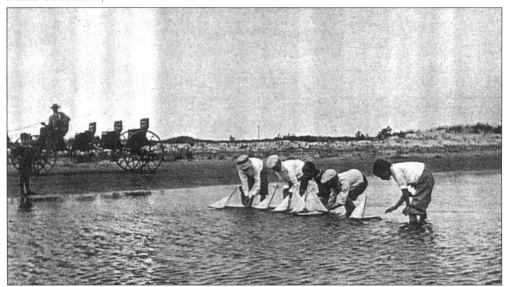

SAILBOAT RACES. These boys line up their sailboats and get ready for the big race. The driver of the ever-present, three-seat carriage patiently waits for the children to wear themselves out before going back to the clubhouse. (Courtesy of Robert Stout and the Eastern Shore of Virginia Historical Society, Wallops Island Collection.)

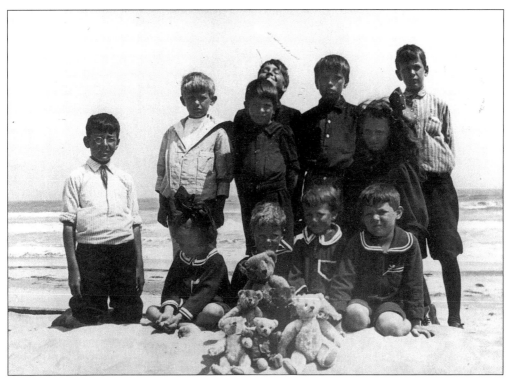

TEDDIES GALORE. These 11 children have gathered their teddy bears for a photo opportunity. Notice how the children are dressed in clothes that do not seem conducive to a fun day on the beach. (Courtesy of Robert Stout and the Eastern Shore of Virginia Historical Society, Wallops Island Collection.)

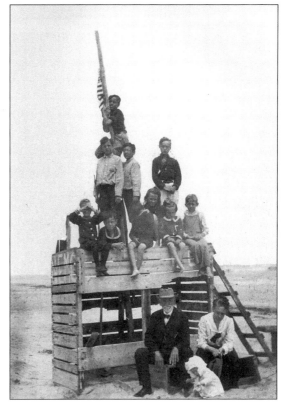

KING OF THE STAND. The boy on the top of the stand hugs a pole with an American flag attached to it. He looks as though he may be of Native-American descent. The couple at the bottom of the stand sit with a baby fully covered and protected from the sun, although not the sand. (Courtesy of Robert Stout and the Eastern Shore of Virginia Historical Society, Wallops Island Collection.)

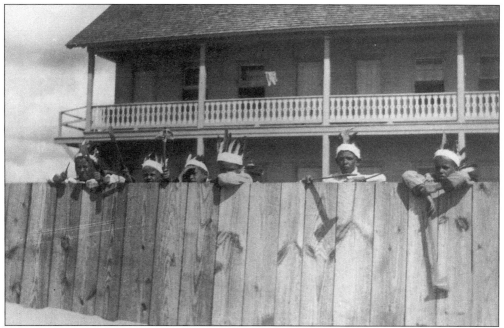

NATIVE AMERICANS. These boys pose behind a fence in their Native-American garb, including fierce looking tomahawks. Curiously absent are any cowboys in this photo. The massacres of Native Americans in the area took place in late 1622 and 1644, and had long since passed at the time of this photo. (Courtesy of Robert Stout and the Eastern Shore of Virginia Historical Society, Wallops Island Collection.)

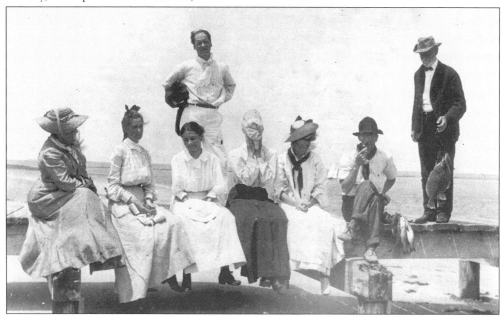

WAITING FOR A RIDE. A group sits on the dock relaxing or waiting for a seaside skiff to come and take them for ride. One man has what looks like a flounder. The shy woman in the middle didn't want anyone to take her picture! (Courtesy of Robert Stout and the Eastern Shore of Virginia Historical Society, Wallops Island Collection.)

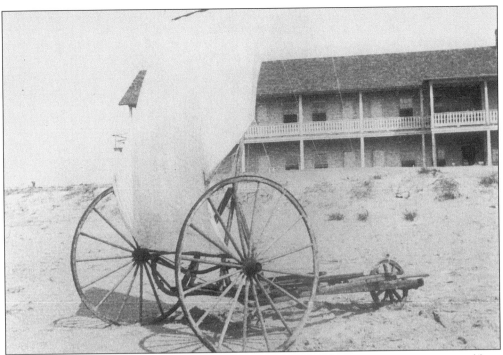

WAGON SAIL. Although we are uncertain as to the name of this invention, it was created by a family visiting the shore during the summer. It probably worked well on the hard sand down by the shore and looks fun to ride. (Courtesy of Robert Stout and the Eastern Shore of Virginia Historical Society, Wallops Island Collection.)

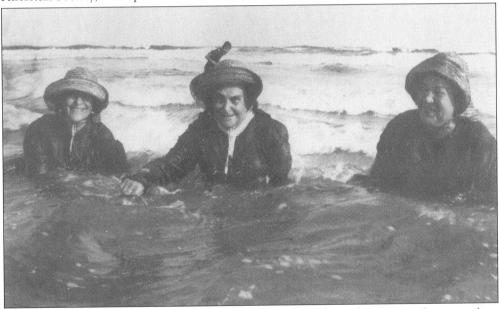

WOMEN IN THE SURF. These women are having a nice cool dip in the water in their straw hats and full length suits, which can be seen billowing behind the women on the left. A boy in the background tries to duck as the photograph is taken. (Courtesy of Robert Stout and the Eastern Shore of Virginia Historical Society, Wallops Island Collection.)

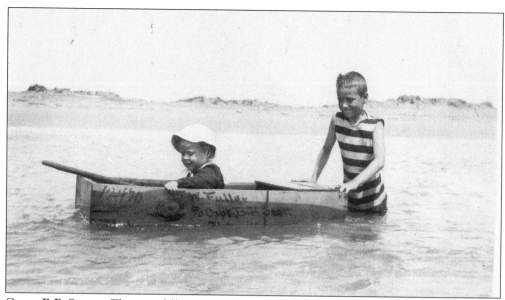

Capt. B.F. Scott. This cute fellow enjoys a ride in Capt. B.F. Scott's little boat. Scott was the caretaker of Wallops Island. The bathing suit the boy is wearing is similar to the style of outfits worn by wrestlers today. (Courtesy of Robert Stout and the Eastern Shore of Virginia Historical Society, Wallops Island Collection.)

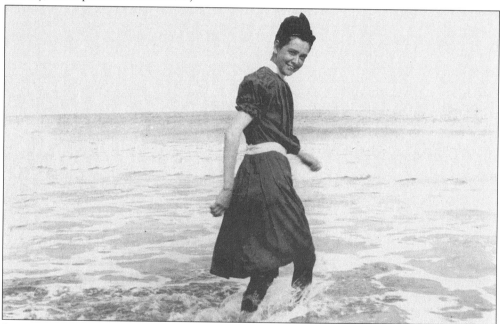

Bathing Beauty. This daring woman heads out for a swim adorned in an itchy wool bathing suit of the 1900s. To complete her outfit she wears wool bloomers, long black stockings, and special lace-up footwear. Of course, proper women of the era wore hats or bathing bonnets to protect them from the sun. This beauty, whose head is wrapped in a bathing bonnet, is truly fashionable as her suit is accented by a white band around her waist along with a matching white collar. (Courtesy of Robert Stout and the Eastern Shore of Virginia Historical Society, Wallops Island Collection.)

Three

1945–1958

The years from 1945 to 1958 were a period of development and permanence as the government started to purchase—instead of lease—land for a fixed time. But the Wallops base was growing so fast that as soon as permanent facilities were erected they were occupied, and construction took so long that by the time buildings were completed, more facilities were needed. These are years, then, that witnessed a building boom, the acquisition of vessels and vehicles for transportation, the procurement of high-performance rocket motors, numerous aerodynamic, flutter, and drag tests as well as wing design and the use of the ramjet, and the development of multi-stage rockets. The initial missile program for Wallops included 12 Gorgans, 36 Tiamats, 10 Supersonic Missiles, and a Ramjet Test Vehicle. These were also the years of reorganization, expansion, the dredging of the channel, and the introduction of various rocket models. NACA purchased the entire island for a little over $93,000, and continued constructing facilities with the aim of conquering supersonic speeds. The administration of the operation did all it could to make the workers content while spending their time on an austere island with little or no conveniences. Fishing and a lounge with an antiquated TV set were the primary sources of recreation. Unless otherwise stated, photos in this chapter are courtesy of Joseph Adams Shortal.

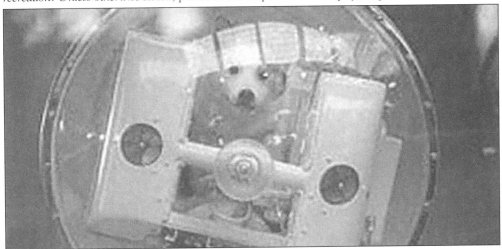

SPUTNIK I AND II. The launch of Sputnik I, Russia's first successful artificial earth satellite, took place on November 4, 1957. This initiated the space age and demonstrated how much America had lagged behind the USSR, even though the three-stage *Vanguard*—which was part of the existing sounding rocket program—had been earmarked to propel us first into the space race. Thus, the DDE commissioned Wernher Von Braun (the renown Army missile man) to convert *Jupiter C* into a satellite launcher. In 1955 the DDE had announced and emphasized the United State's drive in meeting Russia's enterprise with *Vanguard* on the launching pad by December 1957. By then, however, Russia had launched Sputnik 2, called *Laika*.

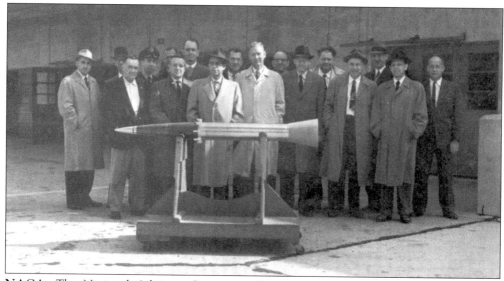

NACA. The National Advisory Committee for Aeronautics (NACA), headquartered in Washington, D.C., was established in 1945 in response to Russia's post-World War II advancements. Wallops Island served as an auxiliary base of Virginia's Langley Laboratory, founded as a test range for guided missiles flight research and to initiate subsonic flights to transonic, and on to supersonic, speeds. Initially, Wallops Island was cloaked in a "need-to-know" basis, though now most of the base is accessible to the general public with proper credentials. However, its formative years of "top secrecy" limited the availability of historical information. Twelve members of NACA, which later became NASA, were representatives of the Army Air Force, the Navy's Bureau of Aeronautics (BuAers), the Weather Bureau, and the Bureau of Standard Smithsonian Institute. In this photo, key members of NASA's Special Committee on Space Technology assemble behind a model of a multi-stage hypersonic rocket vehicle at Wallops in October 1958. Robert Krieger is visible at the far right.

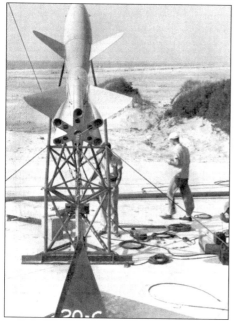

TIAMATS. The Tiamat was the first air-to-air missile launched for Langley's Wallops Island test station, though officially it was called MX-570. Its purpose was to intercept high-flying ground and air launches, though it carried no warhead. Because of Tiamat, Wallops Island came into existence as a test flight base, although Cape Lookout, North Carolina, and Cherry Point, North Carolina, wanted the base as well. This image shows the rear view of the Tiamat with its booster. A series of Tiamats had been developed for testing.

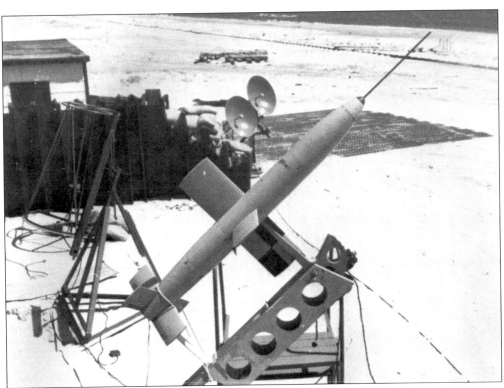

A LARK. Besides the launching of the Tiamat for the Army Air Forces, Wallops Flight Facility also developed the Lark missile in 1946 for the Navy's Bureau of Aeronautics (BuAers). This surface-to-air subsonic vehicle was designed to intercept other missiles. Its specifications included four-way panels and four tail panels similar to the RM-1; the scaled down model (this photo shows a 0.5 scale Navy Lark missile) weighed 125 pounds and was propelled by a single internal cordite rocket motor, though it achieved less than Mach-1 speed.

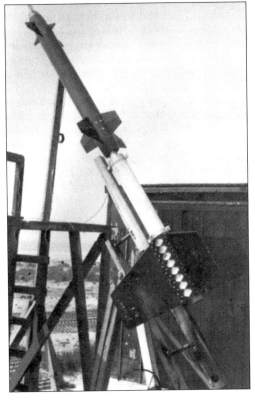

A BELL RASCAL. Still striving for higher Mach numbers, the Army Air Forces hired Bell Labs in 1946 to develop an air-to-ground supersonic missile. After the proposal went through all the channels, and passed all of WFF's initial designs, a 1/6-scale model was created and titled the Bell Rascal, reaching speeds of Mach 1.7. It contained a 5-inch HVAR rocket booster with a 3.25-inch internal motor, and double-wedge wings. Problems arose, illustrating the continuing need for stability and drag studies by Wallops' personnel.

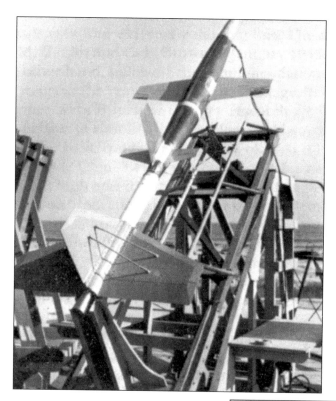

A Douglas XS-3. This rocket model, which followed the Bell Rascal in 1947, was created to gather and study data on aerodynamics transonic range details. The Douglas XS-3 weighed 130 pounds, and was so wisely designed that it was able to reach Mach 1.4 using a 2-stage propulsion system. This prompted engineers at WFF to continue their research programs.

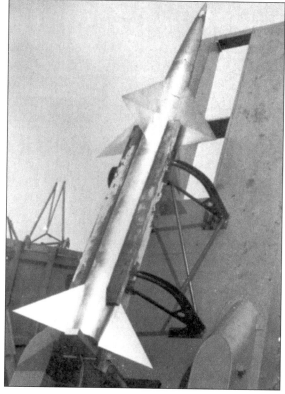

A Sperry Douglas Sparrow. The Sperry Douglas Sparrow, which followed the XS-3, was designed for the Navy. Wallops' prior tests on aerodynamics led to the creation of this complete guided missile system, which contained an internal Deacon Booster. WFF flew six models for testing before being considered a success. The picture here shows a 9/8-scale model on a launcher.

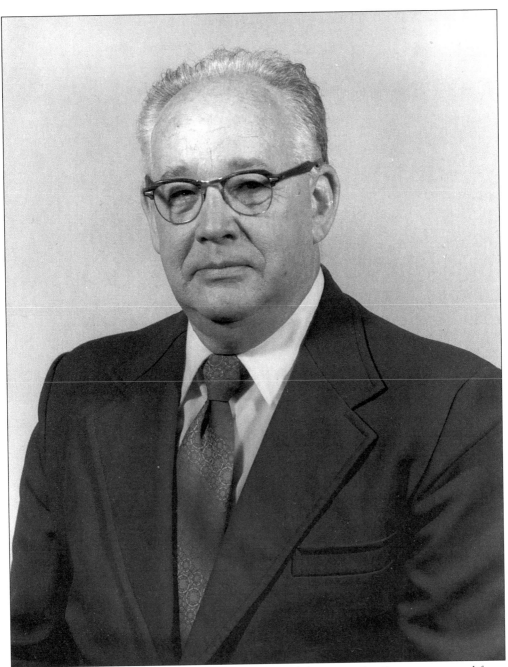

ROBERT KRIEGER. Robert Krieger moved in 1948 with his young family to start a new life on Wallops Island, where he was to become the engineer in charge. Moving from a civilized area to more primitive grounds proved to be too much, so Krieger and his family moved back, only to return again to Wallops Island. Much of the growth of WFF is attributed to both Krieger and Abe Spinak. (Photo courtesy of the Kreiger family.)

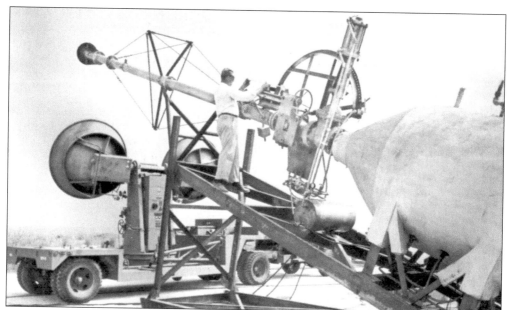

A HELIUM GUN. The Helium Gun was brought on board at Wallops from Langley to measure drag or resistance through all of 1950. WFF was able to acquire the gun since Langley declared it as surplus. Also called the "Popgun," it cost around $5,300 to use and maintain, and required a helium tank to propel a 2-pound model and cradle into space to research Mach 1.6 speeds. Technician Waldorf Roberson is shown here preparing the gun for firing.

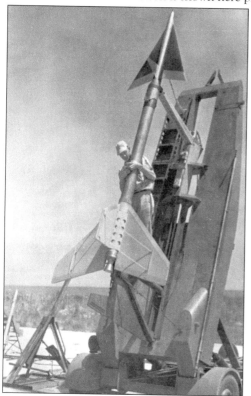

A NORTHROP BOOJUM. The Army Air Forces wanted strategic missile for long-range, intercontinental weapons, so in 1946 they awarded contracts for the development of three strategic missiles. Convair received the nod for the design of the MX-774 (the precursor to the Atlas); North American received the okay for the MX-770 Navaho, which had a ramjet; and Northrop was granted the contract for the turbojet, supersonic MX-775B strategic missile with a deacon booster. Northrop constructed a series of nine 1/14-scaled rockets, of which five yielded valid data. Although considered to be a beautifully designed rocket with a very low drag, it was never completed because ballistic missiles replaced it.

A GRUMMAN RIGEL. This ground-to-ground, long-range guided missile was designed by Grumman Aircraft for BuAer, and had ramjet engines and unswept wings. Three models were successfully flown in 1952. A new, high-speed flutter research vehicle—now designated the D37—contained a telemeter in its nose cone and was able to reach Mach 1.5 with a single Deacon booster. When the Cordite motor was installed in the rocket model, it reached speeds of Mach 2.0 with no evidence of flutter, thus promising that a full-scale model would work just as effectively. In this image, technician George Cutler measures the elevation angle for launching.

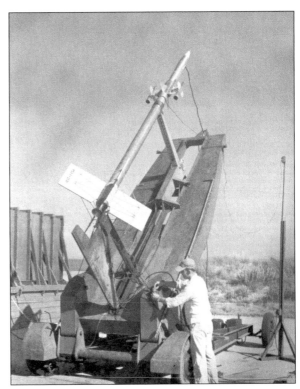

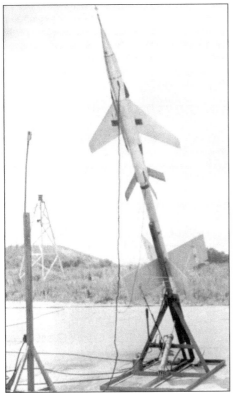

A NORTH AMERICAN YF-100A SUPER SABRE AIRPLANE. This was the first fighter plane developed by the Air Force at Wallops to exceed the speed of sound in its maiden voyage on May 25, 1953. By 1955, it reached speeds of 822 miles per hour. Because of its achievements, this supersonic vehicle was intended to be the main Air Force fighter in close-support operations in Vietnam, as well as serving as the fighter plane for NATO countries. While under development at WFF under the auspices of North American, several tests models were first flown for research on drag, wing flutter, and the overall effectiveness of the plane. This 1953 picture depicts the YF's scaled wings on a D18 flutter vehicle at Wallops.

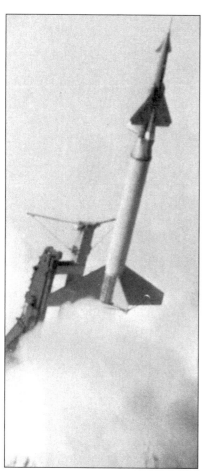

A NORTH AMERICAN GUIDED MISSILE. Named the Navaho, this hypersonic vehicle was a long-range, ground-to-ground missile. Along with the Navaho, WFF tested 13 guided missiles, particularly the Sparrow and Nike, at supersonic speeds. The Navaho was never developed further because it could not reach the desired Mach 2.0 (although there was a lack of research knowledge and facilities for achieving this speed), and also because ICBMs (intercontinental ballistic missiles) came into existence.

A MAN ON A JET BOARD. The principle of balance was tested on jet boards to determine wind effects. Exposing a man standing on a jet board to high winds yielded much needed data, but tests were conducted indoors with guy wires attached to the subject. A nozzle attached to a pre-flight jet issued high-pressured air that was stored in spheres. The burst of air made the man "fly" while strapped to the 19-by-29-inch jet board; a parachute was also attached to him. Later, the project was moved outdoors to increase the wind effect, using a "whirligig" set-up with an overhead rotor. Manufacturers attempted to reproduce this effect for the military in a self-contained machine, but by 1954 interest in the jet board had faded (though it was revised in 1967 for possible use by Apollo astronauts). In this photo, we see Paul R. Hill standing on the jet board outdoors while Abe Spinak (who was to become associate director of WFF) crouches next to the air supply controls.

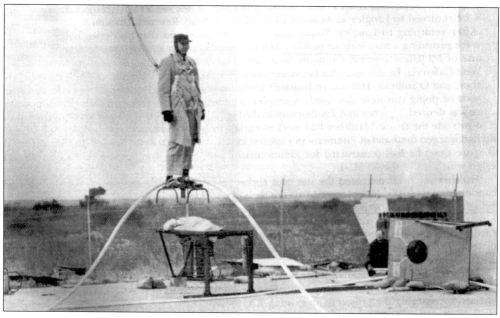

HURRICANE HUGO. WFF was chosen as the site for the development of the Project Hugo Hurricane Photography, as the U.S. Weather Bureau wanted research on hurricane prediction, location, movement, and intensity. From 1954 to 1956, the base generated hurricane studies using WFF's Nike-Cajun sounding rockets, which were sent up four different times. The first launch was July 24, 1956, which went up fine but the recovery package was lost; a second attempt wasn't made until almost 1958, when a Terrier launcher was used. Research was done in such correlative areas as water impact recovery, gust-loads (rocket models exposed to gusty air), analysis of Rawinonde balloon meteorological studies, Leading Edge missile launchers, ballistic missile nose designs, telemeter blackout at hypersonic speed (to test for loss of radio communication at super speeds), and other investigations. Eventually, WFF developed a full-scale weather testing program. The top image shows Harry Bloxom and Durwood Dereng adjusting the first Nike-Cajun hurricane rocket. The bottom photo shows a weather balloon that carries a weather package underneath the balloon. This package measures temperature, precipitation, and humidity, returning to ground by way of remote control radio.

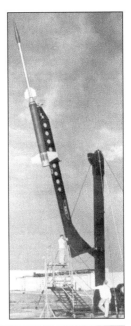

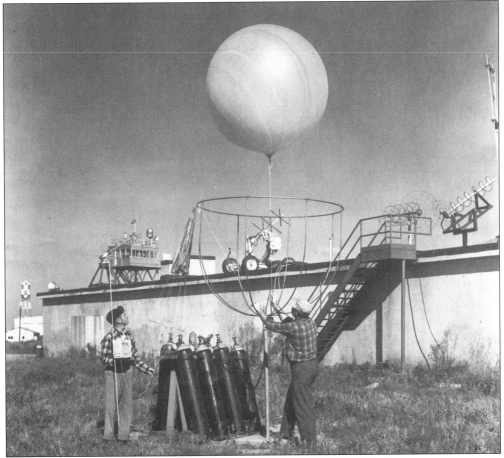

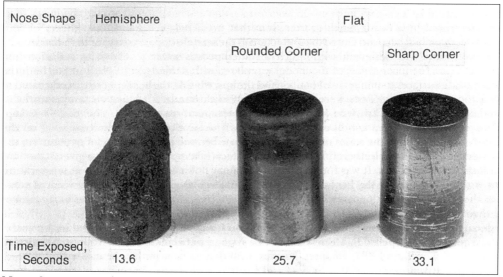

Nose Shape	Hemisphere	Flat	
		Rounded Corner	Sharp Corner
Time Exposed, Seconds	13.6	25.7	33.1

NOSE SHAPES. Besides ongoing studies of aerodynamic resistance, heat transfer, drag, wing stability, winds gusts, and other research done throughout these 12 years at WFF, nose cone studies also became a part of the testing because nose cone research provided information on flow patterns via "shadowgraphs," although tests were later done on nose cones to investigate the dynamic stability of blunt shapes. Cones were exposed to 3,800 degrees at different angles, and tests were also conducted on cones made of different materials, which demonstrated, as well, the viability of metals at different temperatures. This photo shows the effect of 4,000-degree temperatures on nose cones.

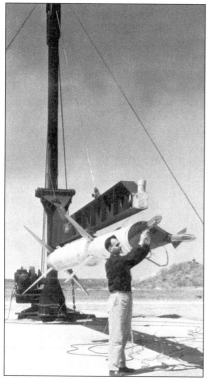

HONEST JOHN NIKE PHOTOGRAPHY, 1956–1958. The "Honest John" ground-to-ground missile was developed by the Douglas Aircraft Company. Its motor was calculated to allow it to reach Mach 10.3 via 4 stages. Honest John's scaled up Nike motor, using double base propellant, was 23.4 feet in diameter, 196.8 feet long, produced 83,000 pounds of thrust for 4.4 seconds, and weighed 3,874 pounds. It was the largest motor at Wallops Island of its day. The 1956 Titan missile was WFF's second attempt at developing an ICBM using a new stiffened cylinder. This didn't work either so it was abandoned, though the information it yielded on heat transfer was invaluable; the model also reached higher Mach numbers than any other rocket of its time. From here, research moved on to studies dealing with the Atlas ICBM's nose cone shape. Because this was much needed and vital information, photography played important role in determining the most viable shape. Likewise, during this period, the base also studied rocket instrumentation via smoke rockets using parachutes supporting the instrument package. The photo shows an Honest John rocket in 1957 with engineer L.T. Chauvin checking it over.

Four
1958–1973

The years between 1958 and 1973 witnessed much change in personnel, testing procedures, rocket designs, landscape, and organizational structures. This was a period of growth for both NASA and Wallops Island, which became the "golden haired boy" of the federal space agencies. Through decades of hard work, WFF gained a reputation for its brilliant scientific teams, its steadfastness in pursuing projects that at first repeatedly failed, and for its innovations in rocket design. The men at WFF understood that they were the originators of what was to be America's space exploration program, and so if they couldn't "get it right," then no one could. No matter how depressing their failures were, or how futile some of their attempts proved, not one on a team that endured the hardships ever gave up. Through them, a host of developments led to the United States becoming the leader of space travel. It didn't come easily or without risk and disasters, nor did it come without step-by-step and trial and error processes. This chapter looks at some of the baby steps taken by personnel at WFF that led up to America's number one spot in universal exploration, and in allowing our country to go where no man had yet gone.

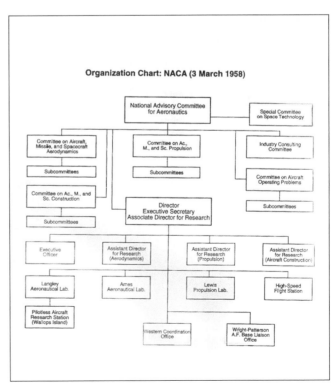

NACA Organization Chart. On March 3, 1958, WFF reported to the Langley Station, which, in turn, reported to the directors of the National Advisory Committee for Aeronautics. On the chart, the Wallops Island base, known as the Pilotless Aircraft Research Station (PARS), is the box located at the bottom left column, with a vertical line connecting it to Langley Aeronautical Lab. If you study the chart, you'll see that the organizational structure of this period seems a little convoluted. (Courtesy of Harold D. Wallace Jr.)

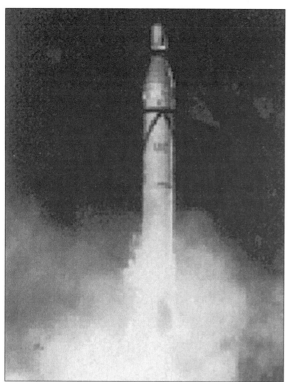

EXPLORER I. When *Sputnik I* beat *Vanguard* into space, President Eisenhower commissioned Wernher von Braun to convert *Jupiter* C to a satellite launcher. On January 31, 1958, *Explorer I* was catapulted into orbit, making it our country's first launched vehicle, and prompting the conversion of NACA to NASA. *Vanguard* became part of NASA. NASA had a major effect on WFF, because after it came into existence, Wallops was endowed with the responsibility of performing critical research test projects for the military in space research. NASA's influence made WFF an operational range for non-military space flight activities as well. (Courtesy of Joseph Adams Shortal.)

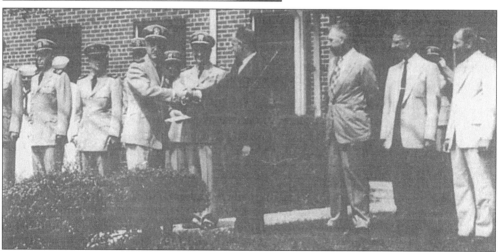

RICHARD KRIEGER ACCEPTING THE AIR STATION FROM THE NAVY. In 1947, Robert L. Krieger was appointed head the Wallops Operation because of his background in "freely falling bodies" and the Wallops missile programs, so he moved his family from the civilized Langley base area to the primitive Wallops Island. After debates between NASA and the Chincoteague Naval Air Station (CNAS) over the purchase and use of all of Wallops Island, the Navy decided to cede the entire land to NASA. This image shows Krieger (in the dark suit), representing NASA, accepting the CNAS on June 30, 1959. This made Chincoteague residents more receptive to NASA because it meant an increase in their economy. At this time, under Krieger, WFF employed 25 Navy and 760 civilian employees. Thus, 1958 marked the beginning of civilian employment. (Courtesy of Joseph Adams Shortal.)

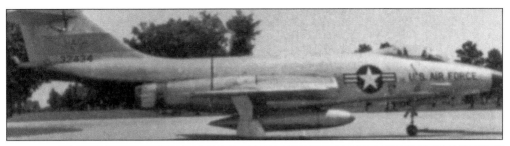

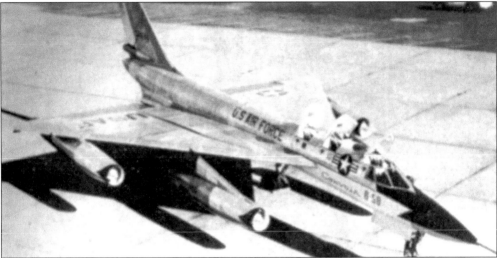

SONIC BOOM SEQUENCE OF EVENTS. On September 23, 1959, the town of Chincoteague experienced the effects of a sonic boom, which broke plate glass windows in a colonial store when an F-101—on its third pass—flew at Mach 1.22 at 25,000 feet with the purpose of gathering information on breaking the sound barrier. NASA paid for the glass damage. Sonic booms are caused by shock waves emitted at supersonic speeds that extend to the ground and thus sound like a massive explosion. Because of its fine reputation as a test site, Wallops Island was selected as the base to build a supersonic transport at Mach 3. Testing was conducted in two phases: the first on September 23, 1958, and then again on October 9, 1958. Six passes were made during the second phase at Mach 1.13–1.40 at altitudes of 25,000 feet and 40,000 feet. TOP: A F-101 in sonic test studies from September to October 1958. MIDDLE: A Convair B-58 at sound breaking speeds on August 6, 1959. BELOW: A Chance Vought F8U-3. (Courtesy of Joseph Adams Shortal.)

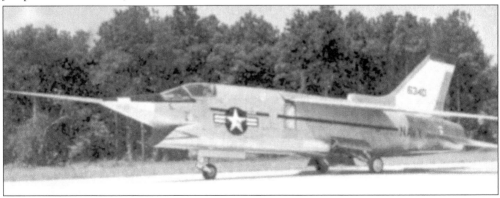

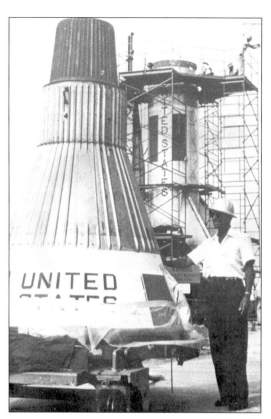

MERCURY. *Mercury* was an important project for Wallops because it set the stage for future testing of vehicles that would reach outer space. One of the functions of WFF was to study the dynamics of the capsule's stability and aerodynamical heating, as well as the safety of the astronauts riding in them. Little Joe Booster was developed especially for *Mercury*, and through its use, WFF tested 26 full-sized scale capsules and 28 scaled-down models. Although *Mercury* was designed without a parachute for the astronaut, the capsule did have other safety features, such as a parachute for the upper canister for safe splash down along with a reserve capsule, a special heat shield around for extremely high temperatures, an escape system, and a special unlock system. *Mercury*'s nose cone, which brought into existence other similarly designed capsules, was researched at Wallops Island from 1955 to 1957. (Courtesy of Joseph Adams Shortal.)

MERCURY'S CAPSULE. The 1958 *Mercury* analyses at WFF had the specific goal of putting humans into space, with tests focusing on *Mercury*'s launch escape systems. The explosion of large boosters was not uncommon back then. Wallops instituted the tests that were eventually carried over to Cape Canaveral for launching, but initially these tests centered on dropping models of varying complexities, from balloons to C-130 aircraft. Some of the aspects of the safety mechanisms consisted of solid fueled rockets attached to the tops of spacecrafts via towers, along with reducing the solid fueled motors from seven to four, which eventually allowed Little Joe booster to hurdle *Mercury* 100 miles. (Courtesy of Harold D. Wallace Jr.)

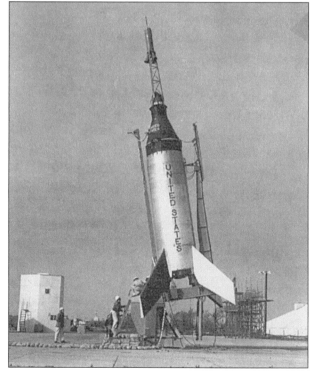

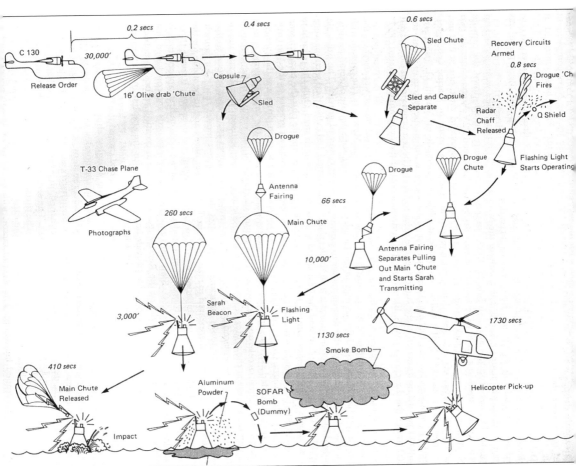

THE PROTOTYPE OF MERCURY. The Mercury Manned Satellite Project placed the United States first in the manned spacecraft studies. Into orbit around earth through WFF's scaled-down and full-sized models, *Mercury's* 1959 prototype was designed for one astronaut—who barely fit inside—to ride into orbit atop a nose cone that replaced an Atlas ICBM ballistic missile. In the sequence of events featured here via radar tracking, the capsule first is dropped from the airplane; the drogue chute opens; then the major chute opens, at which time the capsule drops into the water, where a helicopter would pick it up. The success of the *Mercury* didn't happen overnight; instead, a series of trials was done, and many at first failed. (Courtesy of Harold D. Wallace Jr.)

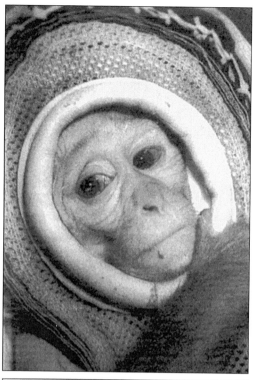

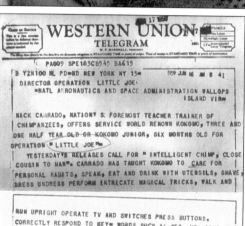

MISS SAM MONKEY. To determine the effects of outer space on humans, particularly high-stress reactions, tests first were conducted on the monkeys Sam and Miss Sam on January 21, 1960. The first flight on December 4, 1959, delivered Sam to an altitude of 53 miles, while Miss Sam (see photo) was comported on a contoured couch on January 21, 1960. WFF used Little Joe 1B booster to launch the capsule. The primates brought forth over 100 photographers from every known media, along with various celebrities—some who became known as "Mercury stars." Soon after, in April 1961, Alan Sheppard flew *Mercury Redstone* to 116 miles in a suborbital path, which marked the trip as the first official space travel. The telegram at left was received by the director of operations regarding the chimpanzees for the "Little Joe" Operation. (Photo courtesy of Harold D. Wallace Jr.; telegram courtesy of Abe Spinak's family.)

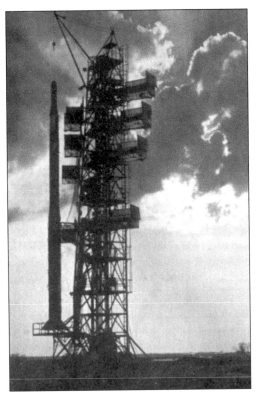

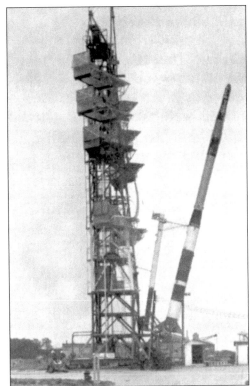

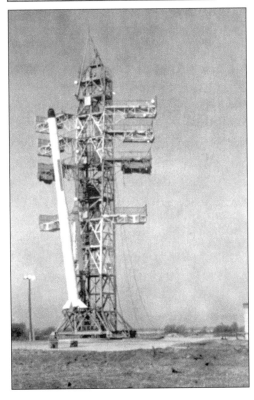

SCOUT ROCKETS. The famous Scout vehicle was developed as a solid-fuel satellite launcher, featuring the newly developed Sergeant five-stage booster to determine the best way for extending speed capabilities of solid-rocket systems. The development of Jupiter Senior (the largest solid-rocket motor) spearheaded the creation of even larger motors for both the Polaris and Minuteman missiles, along with the invention of a new four-stage vehicle that proved to be much less expensive since booster rockets now required one less stage. The first Scout was launched on July 1, 1960, carrying an acceleration and radiation package payload prepared by Langley, and programmed for a probe shot. Scouts were erected on a launcher in a vertical position ABOVE, LEFT: After dummy tests had been completed, Scout, in its actual flight, proved successful except for the third stage motor burning up when the heat shield disintegrated passing through the transonic region. (Courtesy of Joseph Adams Shortal.)

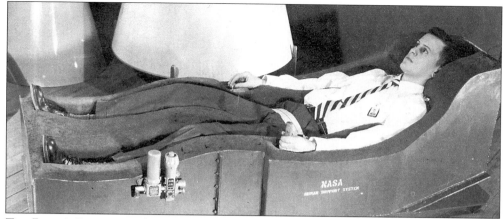

THE PILOT'S POSITION. This image illustrates how an astronaut would lie in a supine position on a 6-foot diameter couch, as it would be constructed across the base of a rocket's cone. All components had to be factored into its construction because the astronaut's safety was at risk. In the end, PARD came up with this design. Alan B. Shepherd Jr. served as the first subject to test out the couch and the first man to complete a suborbital flight on May 5, 1961. Less than a year later, John Glenn was the first astronaut to complete an orbital flight. (Courtesy of Joseph Adams Shortal.)

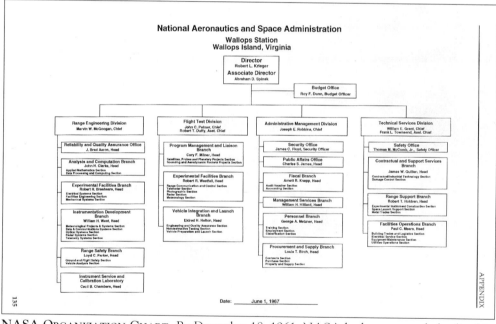

NASA ORGANIZATION CHART. By December 18, 1961, NASA had pretty much finalized its personnel structure, as seen here. In this hierarchy, Robert Krieger serves as the director of the Wallops Station—a key position in the NASA organization—with Abraham Spinak moving up to overseeing the Range Engineering branch. Both he and Krieger devoted a major portion of their time and a chunk of their lives to the success of WFF. Six years later, around 1967, Krieger still held the position of director but Abe Spinak was promoted to his assistant with the official title of "associate director." Notice the four main divisions and their personnel reporting to Krieger and Spinak, some of whose names are recognizable even today. (Courtesy of the Spinak family.)

SEASON'S GREETINGS. This 1962 holiday memo relays a telegram that was received from NASA Headquarters showing appreciation to all the employees along with a message from Krieger himself, wishing everyone a happy holiday. (Courtesy of Abe Spinak's family.)

NASA - Wallops

December 19, 1962

MEMORANDUM For Staff

Subject: Season's Greetings

1. The following telegram has been received.

"SEASONS GREETINGS TO ALL NASA EMPLOYEES"

"AS WE APPROACH THE CHRISTMAS SEASON, AND THE END OF OUR GREATEST YEAR OF ACHIEVEMENT, ALL OF US IN NASA ARE ENTITLED TO A FEELING OF PRIDE IN THE SUCCESS OF OUR EFFORTS.

"DURING 1962 WE HAVE ADVANCED RAPIDLY TOWARD ACHIEVING PRE-EMINENCE FOR THE UNITED STATES IN SPACE. THIS IS SIGNIFICANT FOR MANY REASONS, BUT THE MOST IMPORTANT OF THESE, PERHAPS, IS THE FACT THAT YOUR EFFORTS CONSTITUTE A VERY REAL CONTRI-BUTION TOWARD THE ULTIMATE REALIZATION IN THE WORLD OF THE TRUE MEANING OF CHRISTMAS - - PEACE ON EARTH AND GOOD WILL TOWARD MEN. WE ARE GRATEFUL TO YOU ALL FOR THE SPIRIT OF SELFLESS TEAMWORK WHICH HAS MADE POSSIBLE THE SUCCESSES WE HAVE HAD, AND EXTEND TO YOU OUR WARMEST WISHES FOR A PLEASANT AND HAPPY HOLIDAY SEASON.

JAMES E. WEBB
ADMINISTRATOR

HUGH L. DRYDEN
DEPUTY ADMINISTRATOR

ROBERT C. SEAMANS, JR.
ASSOCIATE ADMINISTRATOR"

2. During the past year we have passed many significant milestones at this Station, the last of which was the successful orbit of EXPLORER XVI. May I extend to you my sincere thanks for a job well done!

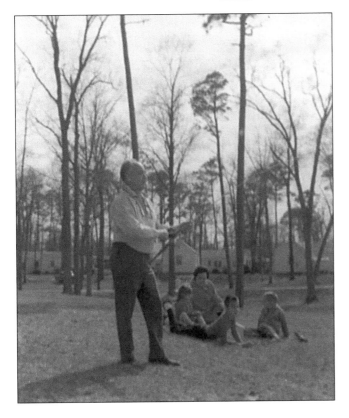

ROBERT KRIEGER. Robert Krieger relaxes with his family and flies a kite in this photograph. It was taken in the early 1960s according to his daughter Lynn Hines. (Courtesy of Robert L. Krieger's family.)

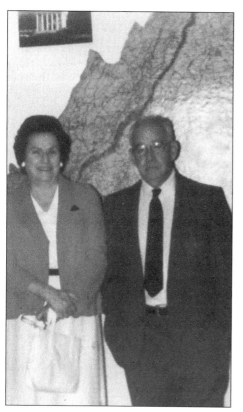

MR. AND MRS. ROBERT KRIEGER. This 1964 photo depicts Krieger and his wife at the dedication of the Eastern Shore Community College; the school was initially located in a World War II housing unit for Navy personnel. Krieger was a prime mover in founding the two-year branch of the University of Virginia, and he is credited for his dedication to higher education—particularly for establishing post-secondary studies in the shore. On July 1, 1971, the college became a vital part of Virginia's community college system and was renamed the Eastern Shore Community College. The campus continued at the Wallops Island location until 1974, when it moved to the new campus at Melfa, Virginia. Today Richard E. Jenkins—who had remained friends with Krieger until the latter died—is president of the Community College. Jenkins started in 1968 as an assistant professor of history, then was promoted to dean of student services in 1972. He was promoted and appointed to the college's presidency in 1996, and he continues in this position today. (Courtesy of the Krieger family.)

MR. AND MRS. ABRAHAM D. SPINAK. Spinak is shown here with his wife, Ruth, at a function at Wallops. Spinak was always good natured and participated one Secretary's Day in a play. During his career he received an honor for the NASA Equal Employment Opportunity (EEO) Medal for "contribution to the formation and implementation of the goals of NASA's EO Programs." Mr. Spinak was specifically honored for his leadership in the EO Council during 1980–1981 as well as his contributions to NASA's program of "identifying, hiring and placing many minority and female engineers and scientists in NASA's roles." (Courtesy of the Spinak family.)

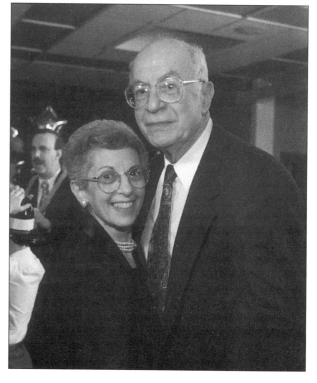

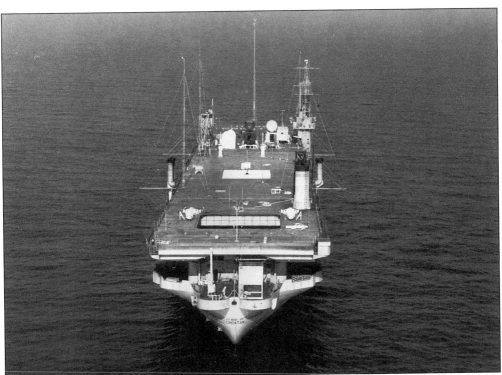

THE CROATAN. This ship went on a mobile mission loaded with instrumentation to fire and test various rockets built at Wallops Island. The expedition was supported by the International Geophysical Year Program. The tour included stopping in the Panama Canal and traveling the West Coast of South America. Along with various scientific instruments the *Croatan* also carried jeeps. (Courtesy of the Spinak family.)

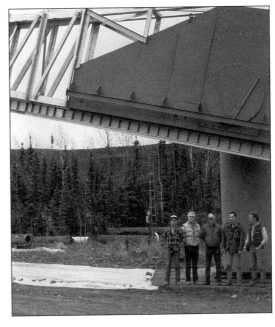

AN AML LAUNCHER. This photograph was taken at the Poker Flats Research Range, located outside of Fairbanks, Alaska. The research range, which is owned by the University of Alaska, is the home of this launcher, which sports a truss made on Wallops Island. Technicians from WFF travel to Alaska in the summer for maintenance to the launchers and return in the winter for the actual launch of the Black Brant rockets. The Brants are shot into the aurora borealis and gather data so scientists can study the reasons this phenomena occurs. The men shown here, including Larry Rovin from Wallops (wearing a green military jacket), stop to pose after completing the installation of the truss. (Photo courtesy of Larry A. Rovin.)

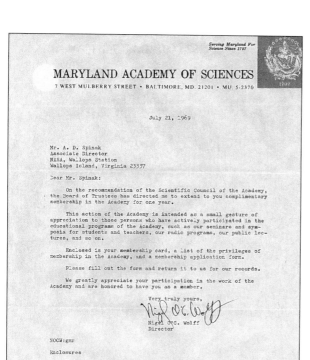

Serving Maryland For
Science Since 1797

MARYLAND ACADEMY OF SCIENCES

7 WEST MULBERRY STREET • BALTIMORE, MD. 21201 • MU. 5-2370

July 21, 1969

Mr. A. D. Spinak
Associate Director
NASA, Wallops Station
Wallops Island, Virginia 23337

Dear Mr. Spinak:

On the recommendation of the Scientific Council of the Academy, the Board of Trustees has directed me to extend to you complimentary membership in the Academy for one year.

This action of the Academy is intended as a small gesture of appreciation to those persons who have actively participated in the educational programs of the Academy, such as our seminars and symposia for students and teachers, our radio programs, our public lectures, and so on.

Enclosed is your membership card, a list of the privileges of membership in the Academy, and a membership application form.

Please fill out the form and return it to us for our records.

We greatly appreciate your participation in the work of the Academy and are honored to have you as a member.

Very truly yours,

Nigel O'C. Wolff
Director

NOCW:gmr

Enclosures

SPINAK ACADEMY MEMBERSHIP. Spinak participated in the education programs of the Maryland Academy of Sciences. The academy extended a complimentary membership to him for his work and active participation in the programs. (Courtesy of the Spinak family.)

SOUNDING ROCKETS. These rockets are being prepared for the "total eclipse mission" by Wallops personnel. The rockets will bring back data regarding the eclipse. (Courtesy of NASA and Wallops Flight Facility.)

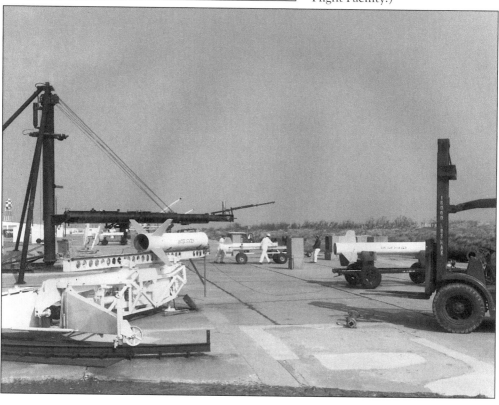

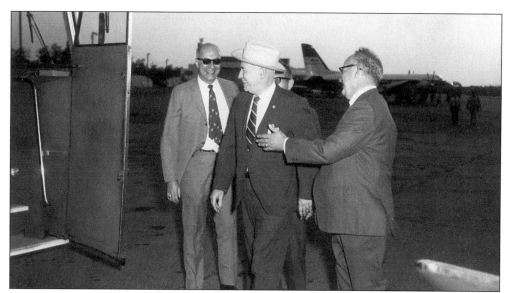

HEAD HONCHOS. Dr. Robert Gilruth (center) was the first head of the Manned Spacecraft Center in Houston, which later was known as the Johnson Space Center. Gilruth was known in the early 1960s as "Mr. Space." The director of the Mercury, Gemini, and Apollo programs, he was frequently in Langley, Virginia, when he was with NACA but spent a lot of time in Houston. Abraham Spinak (left) and Robert Krieger (right), chat with Gilruth before boarding the awaiting bus at Wallops Flight Facility. (Photo courtesy of the Spinak family.)

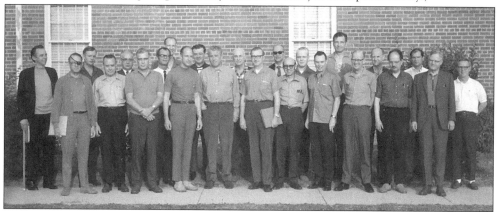

PROJECT COMPLETE. These men pose for a photograph after their project was completed. Pictured from left to right are Ed Schmidt, NASA Headquarters; Dale Myers, A.A., Man in Space Center; Neil Armstrong, astronaut; Jerry Trensynski, A.A., tracking and data; Robert Krieger, director of Wallops; D. Wyatt, administrative office; Robert Jastro, director of the Goddard Institute of Space and Science; Bruce London, director of the Lewis Research Center; George Low, deputy administrator, NASA; Charles Matthews, A.A., applications; Werner Von Braun, director of the Marshall Flight Center; Robert Gilruth, director of the Man In Space Center; Thomas Paine, administration, NASA; A.D. Spinak, associate director of Wallops; John Naugle, D.A.A., Space Science; Julian Scheer, NASA PAO; Oran Nicks, deputy director, Langley Research Center; Ray Kline, administrative office; Arthur Clarke, author; William Pickering, director, JPL; William Shapely, associate department of administration; J.E. Foster, NASA Headquarters; Homer Newell, A.A., Space Science; and Close Farley, NASA Headquarters.

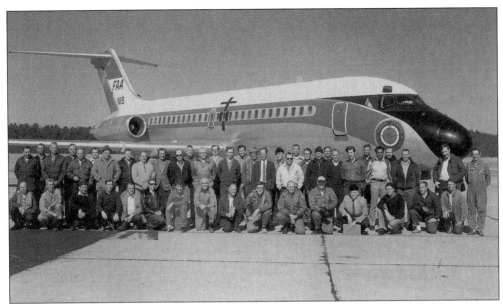

PERSONNEL IN FRONT OF A PLANE. The crew line up for this photo upon completion of the Aircraft Noise Program. This program was done jointly between the FAA and NASA. The purpose of the program was to develop noise standards for aircraft. From these tests the government implemented regulations that are followed by all the airlines today. (Photo courtesy of the Spinak family.)

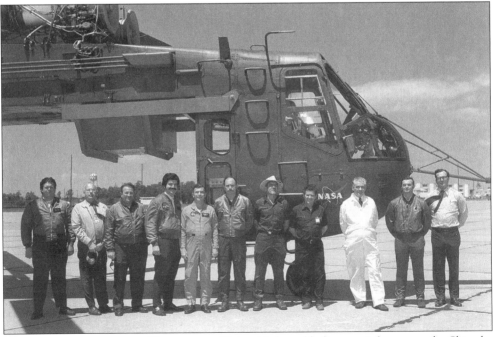

PERSONNEL IN FRONT OF A HELICOPTER. This odd-shaped helicopter is known as the Skirsuky Sky Crane. This type of helicopter is a standard Army brand, and is used today to lift anything heavy, including beams for skyscrapers. Additionally, the Sky Cranes are used for fighting fires by carrying water to the fire. (Photo courtesy of the Spinak family.)

Five
1974–1981

During the years 1974 to 1981, Wallops Island was still being utilized as a launch facility for orbital vehicles as well as suborbital vehicles; the Research Airport at Wallops was used for aircraft noise reduction and runway surface studies. Research for heat transfer and aerodynamics provided the groundwork for unmanned aircraft models, still being tested today.

The Navy Surface Weapons Center in Dahlgren, Virginia, needed to establish a new surface ship weapons engineer facility to supplement its current facilities. In 1980, the Navy signed a Host-Tenant Agreement with NASA to use an existing building for the purpose of long-term projects. The projects that were conducted included engineering studies, the testing of weapons, and combat and battle force systems. The Navy made the decision to use this location indefinitely and five civilian workers and their families were eventually moved to the area.

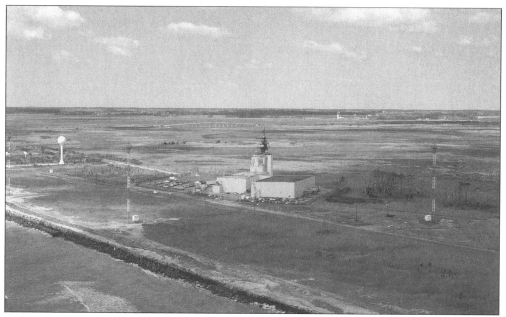

AEGIS OF WALLOPS ISLAND. Throughout the base's progress in developing rockets, balloons, and other projects, WFF also grew physically, resulting in the expansion of the launch pads from one to six, as well as the installation of more sophisticated state-of-the-art instrumentation. Today, space facilities and various structures stretch from one end of the island to the other. Because of the size of the island, other entities partner with NASA and WFF, such as AEGIS and the Coast Guard. AEGIS is pictured here. (Courtesy of NASA and Wallops Flight Facility.)

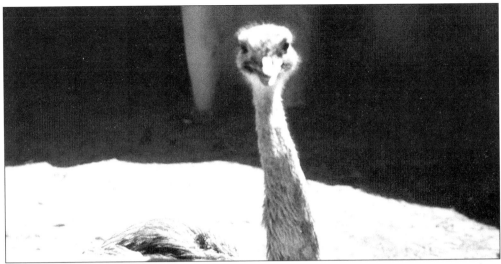

AN OSTRICH. This 1974 photograph of an ostrich came from Abe Spinak's album given to him at his retirement. Upon questioning employees of Wallops, the authors were told that no one has a recollection of the bird ever being at the base. Perhaps Spinak was the only one who saw a bird at Wallops Island other than those with metal wings. It was suggested that perhaps the photo was taken while Spinak was taking part of a project at another location. (Photo courtesy of the Spinak family.)

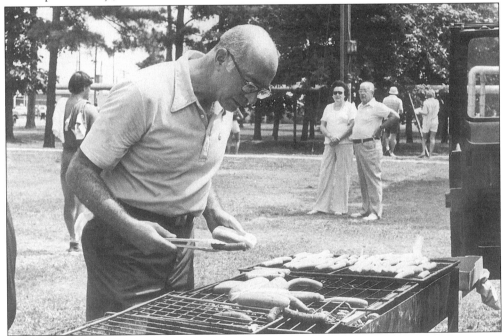

BBQ AT WALLOPS. Abe Spinak lends a helping hand at a summer picnic in 1974 serving hotdogs and hamburgers. The barbeque was given for the Russians who had come over to Wallops Flight Facility by ship. They came to Virginia to ascertain why their atmospheric temperature readings were different from those of the United States. Rockets were fired from their ship and from Wallops' shore to try and find a uniform way in which to take these temperature readings. (Photo courtesy of the Spinak family.)

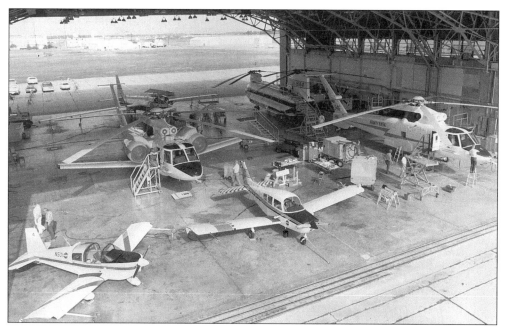

WALLOPS HANGER. A variety of aircraft are shown here in the Wallops Hangar. In the foreground two stall-spin aircraft can be seen; also pictured are a Nasa Army Rotor Systems Research Aircraft (also shown below), a NASA U-2, and a research helicopter. (Photo courtesy of Robert Duffy.)

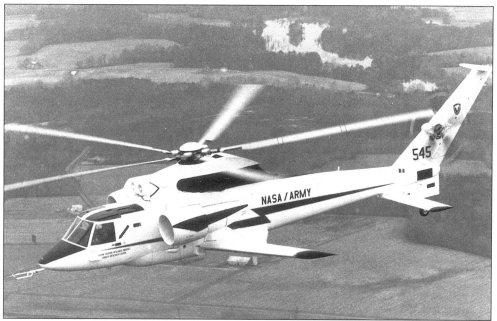

ROTOR SYSTEMS RESEARCH AIRCRAFT. This was the most sophisticated research aircraft and made its first flight as a "compound helicopter-fixed wing aircraft" in 1978, at Wallops Flight Center. NASA worked with the Army on this project. Additionally, two wind tunnels were built for further research and development of advanced helicopter rotor systems. (Photo courtesy of NASA and Wallops Flight Facility.)

THE SOCIETY OF EXPERIMENTAL TEST PILOTS

POST OFFICE BOX 986   LANCASTER, CALIFORNIA 93534   (805) 94...

NASA WALLOPS
FLIGHT CENTER
RECEIVED
APR 1 4 1975
7|8|9|10|11|12|1|2|3|4|5

Wings of Man Dinner

J. H. DOOLITTLE
LIEUTENANT GENERAL
UNITED STATES AIR FORCE, RETIRED
HONORARY CHAIRMAN

10 April 1975

Mr. Robert L. Krieger, Director
National Aeronautics and Space Administration
Wallops Flight Center
Wallops Island, Virginia 23337

Dear Mr. Krieger:

Mr. Neil Armstrong has accepted The Society of Experimental Test Pilots'
invitation to receive its "Wings of Man" Award in recognition, not only,
of his outstanding contributions in the field of aviation and manned
space exploration, but also for the many civic activities to which he
has dedicated so much of his time. The presentation of this coveted
honor will take place on 21 May 1975 during a gala dinner-dance in the
International Ballroom of The Beverly Hilton, Beverly Hills, California.

As Chairman, it is my special privilege to invite you to join the Honorary
Committee we are forming to sponsor this merited tribute to one of the most
outstanding citizens of history.

The proceeds from this event will go to the SETP Scholarship Foundation,
established in 1965 to provide educational assistance to deserving children
of the Society's deceased or disabled international membership. To date,
assistance has been furnished to 26 children and in the Fall of this year
the Foundation expects to provide scholarships for at least 10 students.

There will be a meeting of the Committee in L'Escoffier (8th Floor) at The
Beverly Hilton at 4:30pm on 30 April 1975. At that time we will discuss
our plans to make this an exciting and memorable evening in honoring
Mr. Armstrong and supporting this very worthy cause. Acceptance of this
invitation will not obligate you in any way, other than we would be very
pleased to hear your comments and suggestions, as you join us for cocktails.

I would be extremely pleased to add your name to this distinguished Committee. Please let me know by returning the enclosed response card or
calling, in the Los Angeles area, (213) 936-8100 or, in Lancaster,
(805) 942-9574 collect.

Sincerely,

J. H. Doolittle

Enclosure

Sent regrets 4/15/75 RLK

WINGS OF MAN DINNER. Robert L. Krieger was invited to an awards dinner given to honor Neil Armstrong with the "Wings of Man" award. Kreiger did not attend the function, which was held in Beverly Hills, California, evidenced by his note on the bottom of the correspondence: "Sent Regrets 4/15/75." (Courtesy of the Spinak family.)

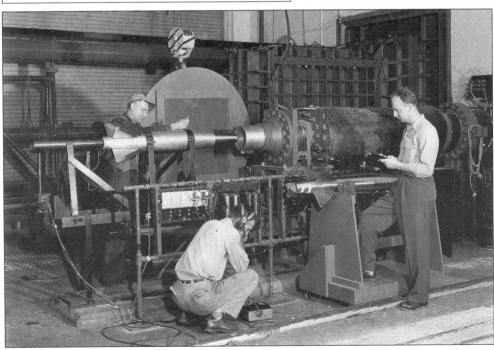

CALIBRATIONS. Robert T. Duffy (right) is pictured here with two other gentleman working on the calibration of wings before they are actually used in a launch. (Photo courtesy of Robert Duffy.)

UK-6. Pictured here is the British satellite being prepared for launch. A photograph of a Scout rocket readied for launching the satellite is shown on p. 2. The satellite will be placed into an easterly circular orbit. UK-6 will gather information regarding high-energy astrophysics. (Photo courtesy of NASA and Wallops Flight Facility.)

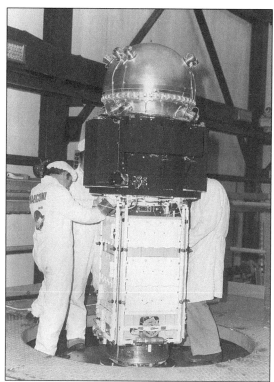

PLANE, 1979. This little plane is a Grumman that was used for spin testing. The two probes that stick on of each wing are to test the air speed and the contraption underneath the tail of the plane is for a parachute if the plane cannot pull itself out of a spin. These tests helped greatly in the knowledge of how a plane reacts when it is in a spin, which helped to increase the pilot's awareness of this type of situation and how best to avoid it from occurring. (Photo courtesy of the Spinak family.)

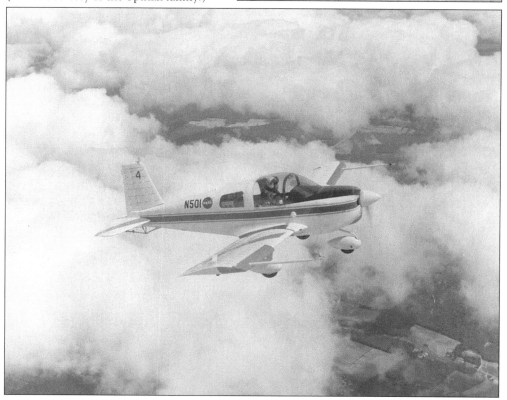

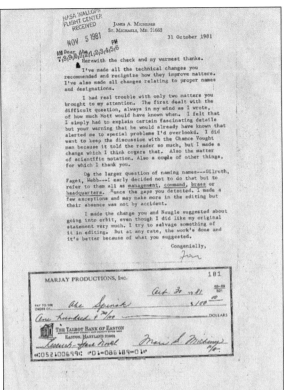

MICHNER LETTER AND PHOTO.
Spinak helped Michner with research for his novel *Space*, as evidenced by this 1981 letter sent to Spinak at Wallops. He spent several hours with Michner discussing the novel, and Michner gleaned Spinak's insight on space and scientific matters. Robert Duffy (see p. 6) is shown below at center with Michner (left) as they are taking a tour of the island. They are leaving the Atmospheric Measurement Laboratory, which has since been moved to another location. (Letter courtesy of the Spinak family; photograph below is courtesy of Robert Duffy.)

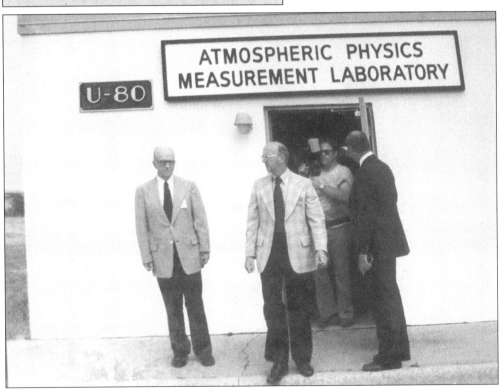

NASA Headquarters Letter. The employees of Wallops Island are applauded for their hard work by James M. Beggs, administrator to Abraham Spinak at the time of his retirement. As is evidenced in this letter to Spinak "[his] outstanding service to the National Aeronautics and Space Administration is greatly appreciated and will certainly be missed." (Photo courtesy of the Spinak family.)

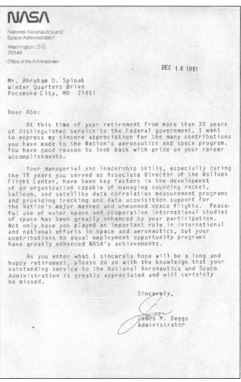

Abe and Ruth Spinak, 1981 Awards Ceremony. Ruth Spinak and Abe Spinak (left) are shown here with another couple at the Honor Awards Ceremony, which was held at Wallops Island on Tuesday, November 3, 1981. Abraham D. Spinak received a certificate and service emblem for his 35 years of service to the National Aeronautics and Space Administration and to the government of the United States of America. Making the presentation is Mr. A. Thomas Young, the director of the Goddard Space Flight Center. (Photo courtesy of the Spinak family.)

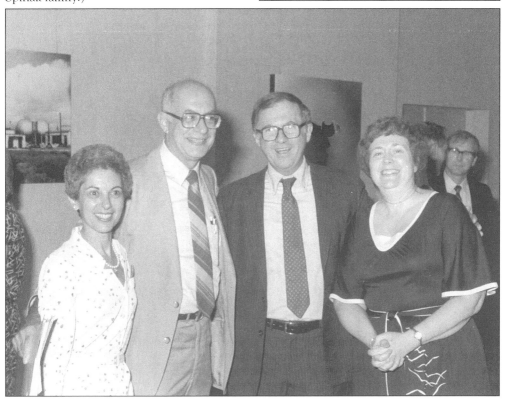

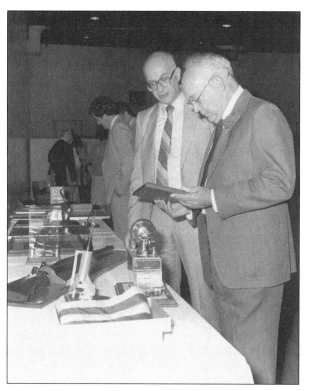

ABE SPINAK AND RICHARD KRIEGER. Spinak (left) and Robert Krieger look over the various trophies and presents Spinak received at his retirement party. Spinak retired from the NASA Wallops Flight Center on November 20, 1981, after almost 33 years of government service. Krieger and Spinak worked closely together for the same number of years. Spinak went on to start the engineering program at UMES and also established the Airway Science Program at UMES. (Photo courtesy of the Spinak family.)

SPINAK'S CARTOON. A co-worker with a good sense of humor altered this cartoon and put Abe Spinak's face on this body. Ruth, his wife, confirmed that even after his retirement in 1981 Spinak had a hard time staying away from the base. (Photo courtesy of the Spinak family.)

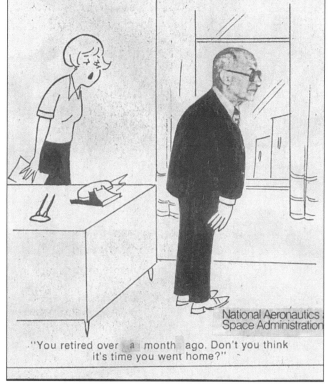

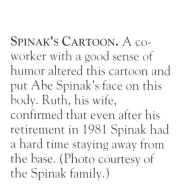

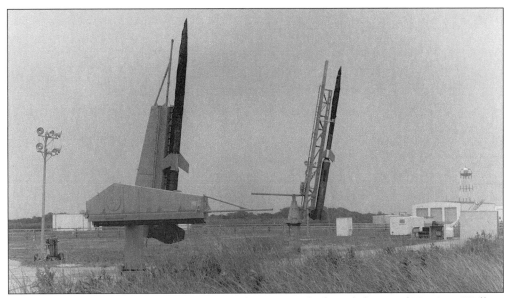

TWO STAGE SOUNDING ROCKETS. These rockets are set for launch from Pad No. 2 on Wallops Island as they await a thunderstorm. The Taurus-Orion is on the left and the Nike-Orion is on the right. They carry experiments to study electric fields above and near thunderstorms. These rockets were part of five vehicle payloads that were being used to measure storm time electric fields from the troposphere to the ionosphere. The other vehicles launched simultaneously were balloons and airplanes. The mission was a major success. (Photo courtesy of NASA and Wallops Flight Facility.)

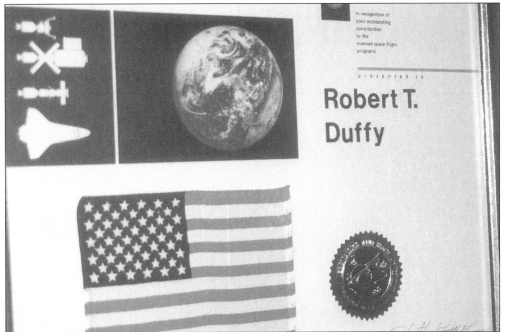

ROBERT T. DUFFY MANNED SPACE FLIGHT PROGRAM. Duffy received this plaque in recognition of his service to the manned flight programs. The flag shown in the photograph was flown aboard the Skylab Space Station. (Courtesy of Robert Duffy.)

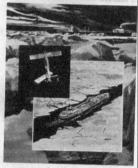

DOCTORATE DEGREE FOR KRIEGER. Krieger received an honorary doctorate degree of engineering from the University of Maryland Eastern Shore, and a plaque honoring his time at Wallops Island when he retired in 1981. (Courtesy of the Krieger family.)

Doctorate Awarded Wallops Center Director

Robert L. Krieger, director of NASA's Wallops Flight Center, received an honorary Doctorate of Engineering at commencement ceremonies held at the University of Maryland Eastern Shore in Princess Ann, Md. May 21, 1978.

Krieger began his career with NASA's predecessor, NACA, and continued thereafter to devote his talent to the expansion of knowledge and technology in the fields of aeronautics and space. He has made outstanding contributions to the development of instrumentation technology, rocket launch facilities and techniques, application of space technology to Earth studies, and to the development of programs of international cooperation in space efforts.

In a letter to the university acknowledging his award, Dr. Krieger said: ". . . I am kept humble only by the sure knowledge that any honor I receive is mostly because I have always had a number of very good people working hard to make me look good!"

He added, in a separate memorandum to the Wallops staff: "Since I've only really had one job in my whole life, and you are the only group of people I have ever had the privilege of directing, I am fully aware that the great work of the Wallops team is what got me the award—and I am truly grateful to you for it."

Satellite to Study the World Oceans

NASA launched Seasat-A, the first satellite to study the world's oceans, from the Western Test Range, Vandenberg Air Force Base, Lompoc, Calif., June 26, 1978. Seasat-A, a "proof-of-concept" mission, will be used to determine if microwave instruments scanning the oceans from space can provide useful scientific data for oceanographers, meteorologists and commercial users of the seas. The spacecraft will send back information on surface winds and temperatures, currents, wave heights, ice conditions, ocean topography and coastal storm activity.

Spacewatcher—How the recently launched Seasat spacecraft will help locate sea ice and sea leads (navigable openings in ice), in an effort to provide safe passage for ships at sea. Seasat will return volumes of data to Earth in its continuous scanning of the world oceans.

An Atlas-Agena launch vehicle sent Seasat-A into a near circular polar orbit 800 kilometers high. The spacecraft will circle the Earth 14 times a day and its instruments will sweep across 95 percent of the oceanic surfaces every 36 hours, providing oceanographers with their first synoptic, or worldwide, observation of the oceans. The spacecraft has all-weather capability, and can see as well at night as in the daytime.

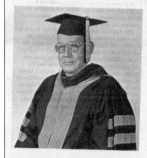

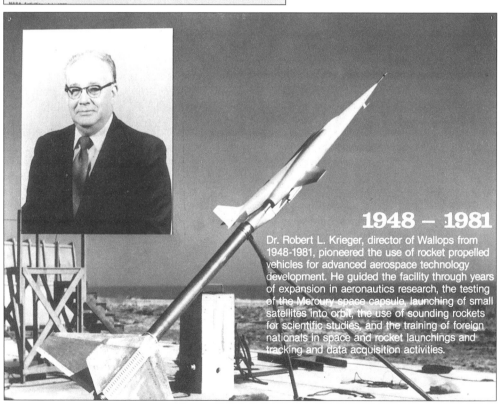

1948 – 1981

Dr. Robert L. Krieger, director of Wallops from 1948-1981, pioneered the use of rocket propelled vehicles for advanced aerospace technology development. He guided the facility through years of expansion in aeronautics research, the testing of the Mercury space capsule, launching of small satellites into orbit, the use of sounding rockets for scientific studies, and the training of foreign nationals in space and rocket launchings and tracking and data acquisition activities.

Six
1982–2000

Wallops Island consolidated with Goddard Space Flight Center in 1982, after which Wallops Flight Facility became NASA's main place for suborbital programs. Academic and government programs continued to be supported along with projects using scientific aircraft, balloons, and sounding rockets to help with research of the earth and space environment and with all areas of the atmosphere.

At present, Wallops Island consists of the Main Base, Wallops Island, and Wallops Mainland. It covers a total of 6,200 acres and 84 major facilities, complete with Wallops Research Airport, aircraft hangars, research laboratories, payload and rocket assembly buildings, machine shops, operations and instrumentation control facilities, and launch complexes.

One of the organizations that interacts with Wallops is the Coast Guard, whose housing was given by NASA in the 1980s. The Coast Guard serves as an outpost during severe weather. They also support Wallops launch range operations by providing ships to clear hazard areas and recover payloads, as well as issuing notices of impending launch activities.

Wallops is currently in the process of developing a five-year plan to be complete by October 1, 2000.

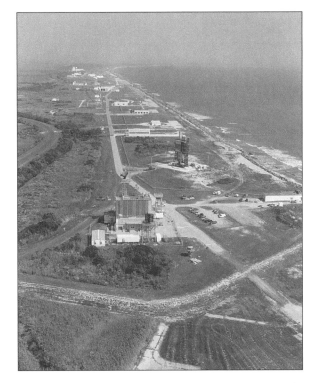

AN AERIAL VIEW OF WALLOPS ISLAND. This 1995 photograph of the island shows the ideal location of the launch facilities. The ocean on the right and the isolation of the island makes it a perfect place for testing rockets. (Courtesy of Nasa Wallops Flight Facility.)

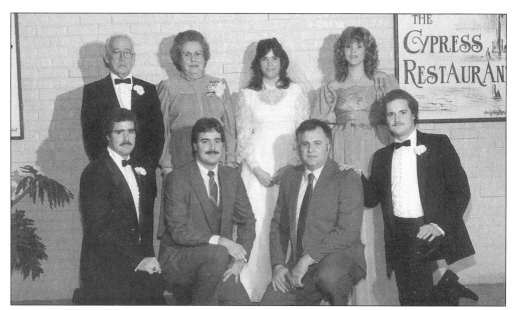

RICHARD KRIEGER AND FAMILY. This early 1980s photograph is of Richard Krieger's family at his daughter Lynn's wedding. With all the "hubbub" happening at Wallops Island, Krieger was still able to take a moment to enjoy time with his family. Everyone is present in the photograph with the exception of one son. From left to right are the following: (front row) William Krieger, John Krieger, Robert L. Krieger Jr., and Richard Krieger; (back row) Richard Krieger, Frances M. Kreiger, Lynn Krieger Hines, and Karen Krieger. The brother not shown is James Ray Krieger, who resides in Atlanta, Georgia. (Courtesy of Richard L. Krieger's family.)

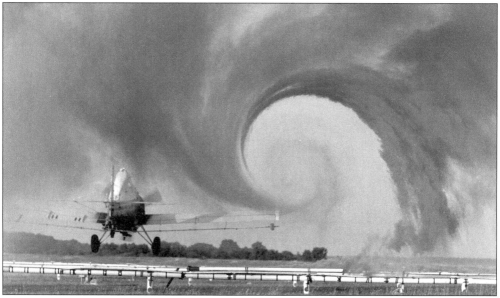

A THRUSH S-2 R-800. This aircraft was used for an aerial applications research program at Wallops Flight Facility. The program was designed to improve the technology used in dusting and spraying crops aerially. The aircraft has a variety of sensors to detect spray and particle drift, dry material and liquid material distribution, and swath guidance. The dust seen in this photograph is bright red in color. (Photo courtesy of NASA and Wallops Flight Facility.)

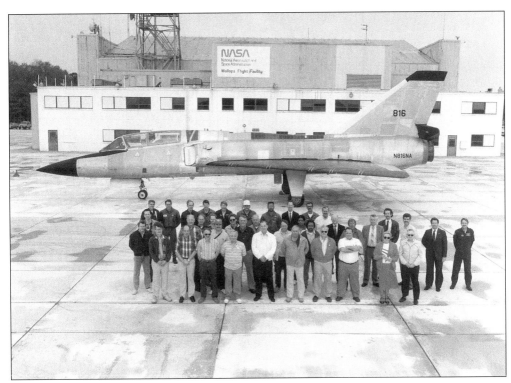

A F-106. Photographs were generally taken after a project was completed. These gentlemen stand in front of a F-106 that was used to fly in the middle of lightning storms to study electric fields above and near the thunderstorms. (Photo courtesy of Robert Duffy.)

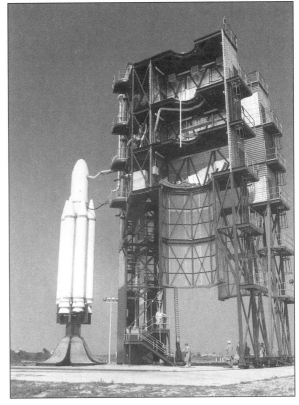

CONASTOGA. This rocket, which was launched in 1995, was the first attempt of a civilian payload and was not part of any Navy venture, although NASA provided support for the launch attempt. The rocket carried a recoverable capsule on board and was to conduct a Micro Gravite Experiment that would occur 12 miles from the shore. Unfortunately, it blew up 40 seconds into the launch. The site has not been used since and the launch pad is being sold. (Courtesy of Nasa Wallops Flight Facility.)

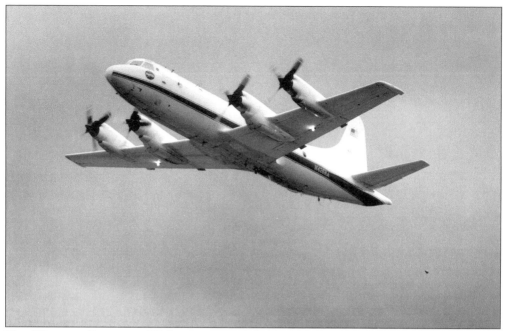

THE WALLOPS PROGRAM. Wallops supports a fleet of airplanes that aid in scientific research. One such endeavor includes having a plane fly to Greenland to measure the icecap to see how many inches it has melted during the year. (Photo courtesy of Robert Duffy.)

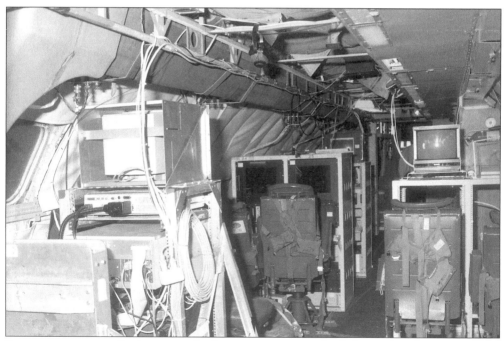

INSTRUMENTATION. Rack upon rack of instrumentation is loaded into the planes, as can be seen here. Many of the instruments are used in conjunction with the satellites to do active measurements. Many of these experiments are part of a large international scientific expedition. (Photo courtesy of Robert Duffy.)

Wallops Aircraft

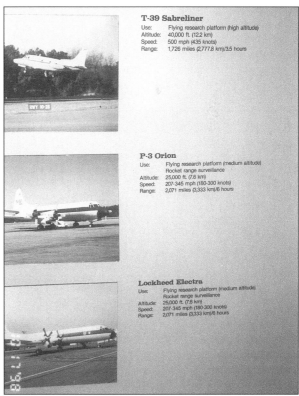

King Air
Use: Administrative flying
Altitude: 35,000 ft. (10.7 km)
Speed: 173-299 mph (150-260 knots)
Range: 1,726 miles (2,777.8 km)/5 hours

UH-1 Huey Helicopter
Use: Flying research platform (low altitude)
Sea/Air rescue
Altitude: 10,000 ft. (3 km)
Speed: 0-115 mph (0-100 knots)
Range: 230 miles (370.2 km)/2 hours

T-39 Sabreliner
Use: Flying research platform (high altitude)
Altitude: 40,000 ft. (12.2 km)
Speed: 500 mph (435 knots)
Range: 1,726 miles (2,777.8 km)/3.5 hours

P-3 Orion
Use: Flying research platform (medium altitude)
Rocket range surveillance
Altitude: 25,000 ft. (7.6 km)
Speed: 207-345 mph (180-300 knots)
Range: 2,071 miles (3,333 km)/6 hours

Lockheed Electra
Use: Flying research platform (medium altitude)
Rocket range surveillance
Altitude: 25,000 ft. (7.6 km)
Speed: 207-345 mph (180-300 knots)
Range: 2,071 miles (3,333 km)/6 hours

WALLOPS AIRCRAFT. Photographs of the aircraft that are used by Wallops Island can be seen in the Visitors Center. The different types of aircraft include King Airs, used to fly the executives to business meetings; UH-1 Huey Helicopters, used for sea rescues; Skyvans, used in the air retrieval of sounding rocket payloads; T-39 Saberliner high altitude research craft; P-3 Orions, used for medium altitude rocket range surveillance; and Lockheed Electras, used for medium altitude rocket range surveillance. (Photo by Bo Bennett.)

73

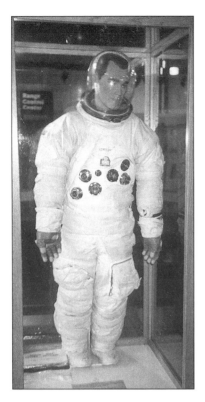

A Practice Suit. This practice suit, actually worn by Lunar Module Pilot Russell Schweickart, can be seen in the Visitor Center. The suit was worn by Schweickart to prepare for the flight of Apollo 9, which took place on March 3, 1969. The suits for the Apollo flights were made more flexible than the original suits by adding "bellows-like joints," which also made the suits easier to work in. (Photo by Bo Bennett.)

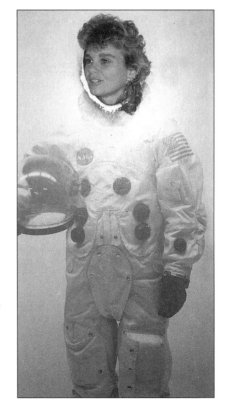

An Apollo Suit. At the Visitor Center, photographs can be taken behind this life size cut-out of an Apollo suit. These suits had extra layers to help withstand the extreme conditions on the moon. They were also more flexible than the original suits of pre-Apollo times. The Visitors Center is open from July to Labor Day daily from 10:00 a.m. to 4:00 p.m.; the rest of the year it is closed on Tuesdays and Wednesdays. A space suit demonstration is given on Sundays at 1 p.m. (Photo by Bo Bennett.)

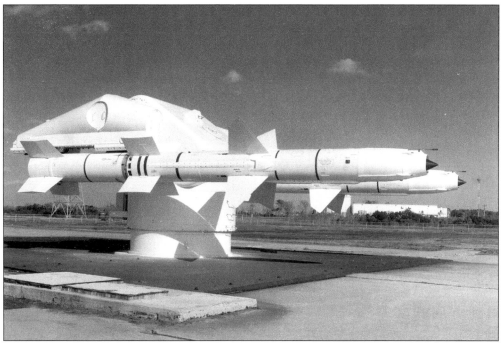

A Vandal Target. Vandals are targets used by the Navy. They are launched six or seven times a year and are non-recoverable targets. A little over 100 have been launched since 1984; prior to that they were used more frequently. Once a Vandal has been launched it flies less than 50 feet above the water and ships shoot at it and are scored. As many as 12 ships will participate in these exercises at the same time to help defray costs. (Photo courtesy of AEGIS.)

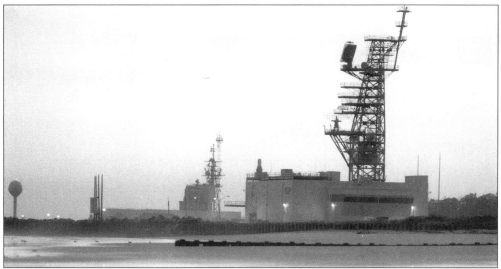

The 1999 Aegis Building. AEGIS is located on Wallops Island and is home to the Navy. The name AEGIS comes from Greek mythology and means "shield of protection." AEGIS was the first name given by Zeus to his invincible goat skin shield, which reportedly protected the mortals from Athens. Today, the Navy uses AEGIS as the shield of the fleet. It is the combat weapons systems on cruisers such as CG-47 USS *Ticonderoga* and DDG-51 USS *Arleigh Burke*. The crews on these ships are trained for anti-ship missile attacks. (Photo courtesy AEGIS.)

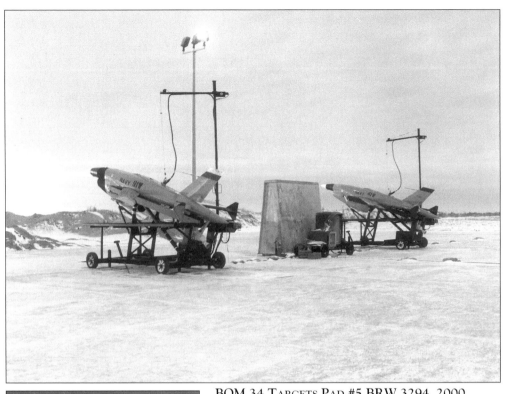

BQM 34 Targets Pad #5 BRW 3294, 2000.
These rockets are slower than other rockets and subsonic. They are a recoverable target, and are capable of reaching altitudes above 40,000 feet and flying as low as 50 feet. The Navy will also shoot at these targets. If the target is not hit it will come down in a parachute and be picked up by a helicopter. (Photo courtesy of AEGIS.)

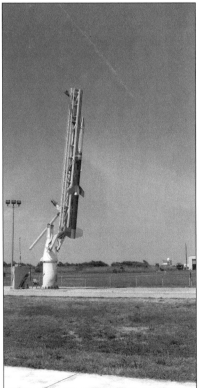

Nike Black Brant Pad #2, 2000. This sounding rocket is used to take measurements. Its flight time is less than 30 minutes—when it is shot up it comes straight back down. The Brant is 65 feet tall and can carry scientific payloads of different weights to varying heights between 300 and 800 miles. They have two parts: a solid fueled rocket motor and payload. The payload is where the information from the experiment is gathered and then sent back to earth. The payload and the rocket separate after the launch; the rocket falls back to earth as the payload continues on and gathers data, and when it has completed its mission a parachute deploys as it reenters the atmosphere and falls back to earth. The whole or part of the payload can be used again for other launches. (Photo courtesy of AEGIS.)

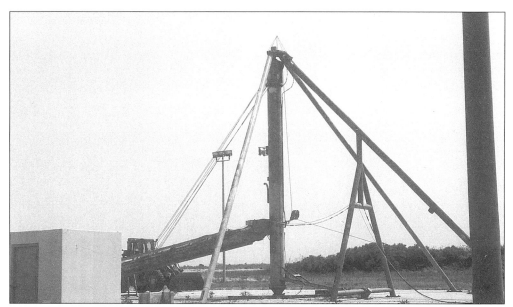

A LAUNCHER. This launch pad is used for launching all types of rockets, especially for the Navy. They send the rockets up and practice what is called "near misses"—they get as close as they can to the rocket without actually blowing it up and then they use the rocket again on their next practice. Sometimes when the rockets can not easily be located, the Navy Seals help out by using their dolphins to locate the submerged rockets. (Photo by Bo Bennett.)

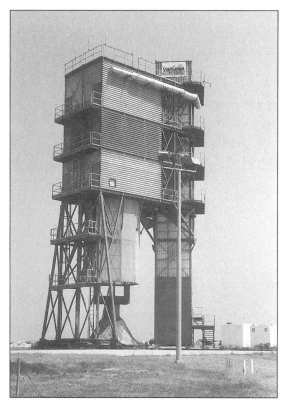

A LAUNCHER. *Conestoga* was launched from this site, which still stands today. The Virginia Commercial Space Flight Authority works with Wallops to promote the use of Wallops for launches. The WFF would like commercial launches to grow to at least six a year and for the airport to be operated on a cost-reimbursable basis. Launches of NASA's sounding rockets continue to take place at Wallops, where range costs are lower. The range supports and is shared with the Naval Air Warfare Center. (Photo by Bo Bennett.)

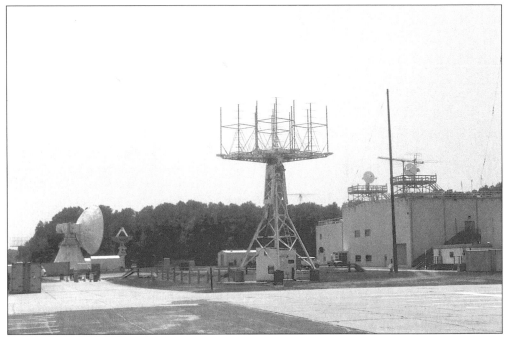

TELEMETRY. The telemetry equipment shown here is used to bring down data from sounding rockets, weather balloons, and satellites. The Telemetry Building houses the Tiros Weather Satellite Command and Data Acquisition Center. Another part of Wallops uses similar devices. Radar Y55 and Y60 are used to track missiles, aircraft balloons, space objects, the space shuttle, and the space station. Most balloons have an aluminized triangle in the corner that serves as a reflector, enabling the radar to track the balloons with better precision. (Photo by Bo Bennett.)

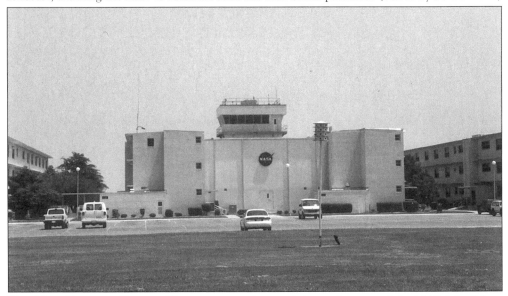

THE NEW CONTROL TOWER. This new control tower is located on top of the NASA building, which houses the monitors that keep track of the shuttle. The older control tower, which is still operational, stands independently from any other buildings along the runway and is still used occasionally. (Photo by Bo Bennett.)

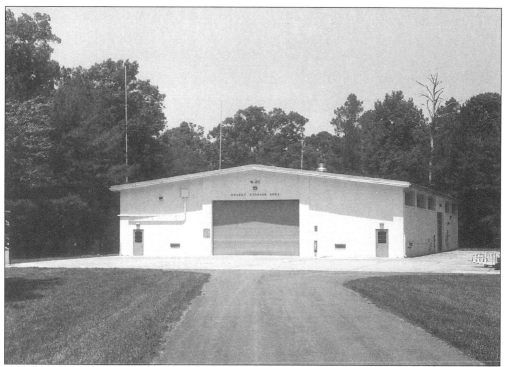

ROCKET STORAGE. The rockets and motors stored in this building are either partially or fully completed, and are kept inside until they are ready to be used. Lightning rods surround the building so when lightning storms occur the building itself will not be hit and the danger of the rockets exploding is avoided. (Photo by Bo Bennett.)

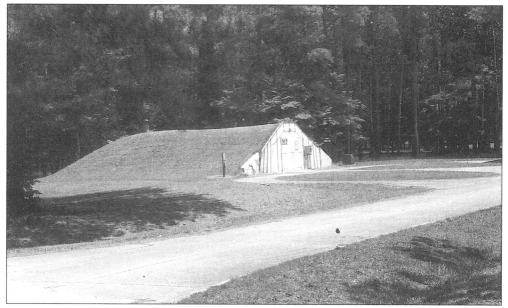

ROCKET MOTOR STORAGE. Originally built in World War II, explosive rocket motors were kept inside these storage units for long-term storage. These areas are climate controlled and are still in use today. The Navy also uses the bunkers for fuel storage. (Photo by Bo Bennett.)

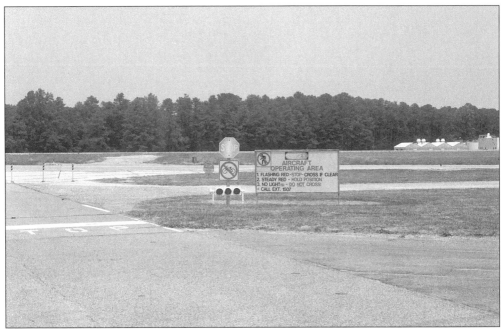

OPERATIONAL RUNWAY. The first road in this photograph is a taxiway for the jets and the second road is the actual runway. Upon approaching this area, if the danger sign is flashing it means to stop for any awaiting traffic. If the signal is red a vehicle must hold its position until the light starts flashing again. The danger sign was posted to warn of potential incoming air craft. If none of the lights are on, the runway cannot be crossed at all. Wallops Research Airport has a total of three runways, including one runway with a friction surface for testing aircraft landings, a control tower, and a fire/safety crash crew. Various agencies use the airport including NASA Wallops planes, the NASA Langley Research Center, the Dover and Andrews Air Force Bases, and other commercial aircraft companies. (Photo by Bo Bennett.)

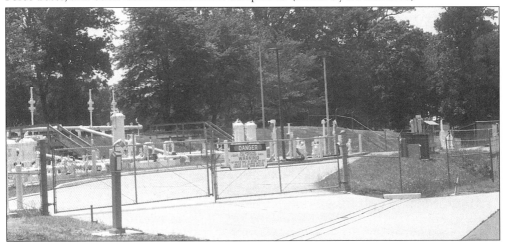

FUEL FARM. This farm supplies the Navy transit aircraft as well as the NASA aircraft with JP4 and JP5 fuel, which is extremely combustible. When a jet needs fuel, one of six fuel trucks is called. The JP4 and JP5 fuel hydrants are kept behind a locked fence for safe keeping. The red post in the left foreground of the photograph is a warning system in case a fire breaks out. This system is environmentally safe. (Photo by Bo Bennett.)

Seven

LANDSCAPE, TRAVEL, AND EXPANSION

Picture a land that over time has had its shoreline eroded by tides and storms, and amassed with sand in some places by those same tides and storms. Imagine an expanse that once housed a country club, with "city slickers" visiting the beach to sunbathe and swim, that through time metamorphosised into a stretch of overgrowth, briar patches, muck and mire, and wetlands that harbor a multitude of stinging insects, particularly mosquitoes that some would swear are as big as crows. This was Wallops Island from the time John Wallop's descendants left the land and the National Advisory Committee for Aeronautics took it over. The landscape has been remarkably altered by civilization. Transportation became more trying as people moved to the area to work at the facility. When NACA came to understand the magnitude of the transportation problem on the lonely island, they devised means of conveying people and equipment from one base to another; yet, it would be years before the landscape of the base would change enough to allow for paved roads, buses, automobiles, and boats. It was only through various phases of expansion that WFF developed enough to make it the world-famous facility it is today.

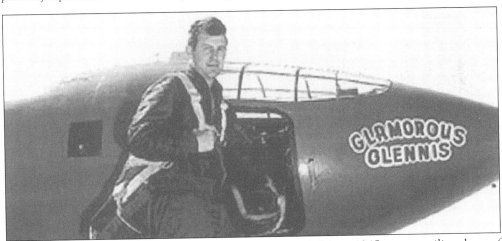

THE X-1. Wallops Flight Facility was established by NACA in 1945 as an auxiliary base of Langley. In its early years, the facility was cloaked in secrecy. Through the efforts of WFF, Charles E. Yeager flew the X-1 through sonic barrier in 1946, while Dr. Robert H. Goddard became famous for launching the first liquid-fuel rocket, which used a combination of liquid oxygen and gasoline. Though unsuccessful, Goddard's research and Yeager's accomplishment served as precursors of modern-day rocketry and space technology. (Photo courtesy of Joseph Adams Shortal.)

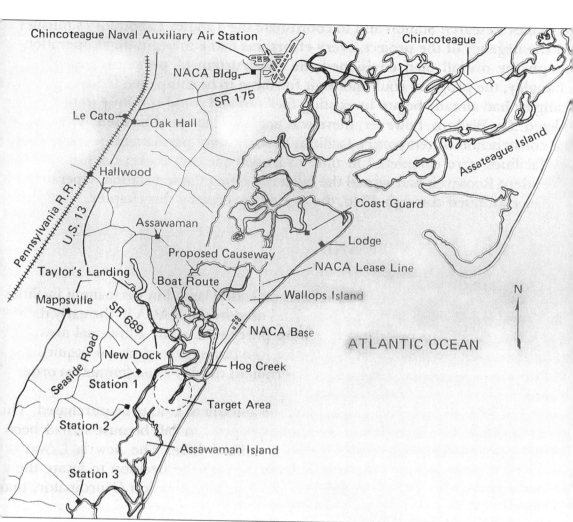

A MAP OF THE BASE. Originally NACA couldn't decide where to locate the test range for the Langley sub-facility; in consideration were various other Carolina bases. In the end, Wallops Island was selected because of the availability of the property. Fortunately for NACA, the Navy simultaneously abandoned the Chincoteague Naval Station, whose location and isolation from the general public made it the perfect facility. Also in its favor was its proximity to the naval base and to Langley, a 60-mile flight range along the barren coast to allow for tracking, and convenience to major cities and the nation's capitol. The down side was that it needed a 2-mile causeway to eliminate transportation problems. The causeway was a long time in coming, and matters were complicated by the fact that the Wallops Island Association still had a presence on the land through its hunting lodge/clubhouse. Nonetheless, Wallops Island got the nod, and temporary facilities were completed in time to launch the first rocket on June 27, 1945, just months after President Roosevelt enacted authorization for establishing the test station. NACA leased and purchased land (via condemnation) for construction of launch and observation pads, along with receiving buildings, tracking stations, and a mainland boat dock, among other necessary structures. (Courtesy of Joseph Adams Shortal.)

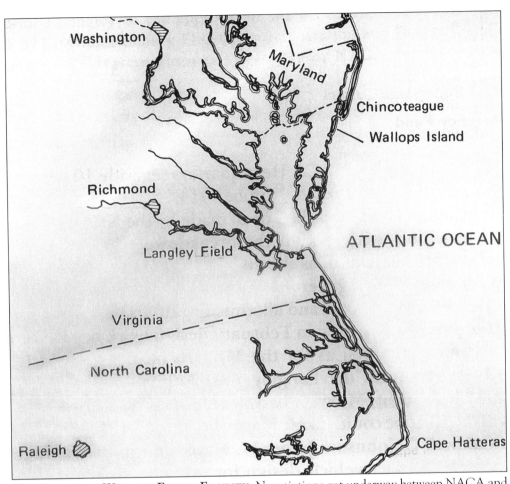

THE LAYOUT OF WALLOPS FLIGHT FACILITY. Negotiations got underway between NACA and Frank Hunter of Norristown, Pennsylvania, who then was president of the Wallops Island Association, for the acquisition of the island's lower 1,000 acres for the construction of additional temporary structures. Although there was some squabbling over that acreage with the Navy, who also wanted to purchase additional land, by May 11, 1945, NACA acquired the 1,000 acres for about $2,000, acquiring Chincoteague Inlet on the north, Assawoman Inlet on the south, Atlantic Ocean on the east, and Assawoman Narrows, Cat Creek, Bogers Bay, and Island Narrow on the west. It didn't take long for NACA to realize that even more land was needed, so on August 9, 1945, NACA "condemned" 84.87 more acres on Wallops Island, and took possession on September 18, 1945. "Condemnation" allowed the government to purchase land to build permanent facilities, since leasing permitted the construction of only temporary buildings. Still, issues weren't settled since the problem of sea range rights arose because NACA thought it already had owned those when they bought the property. About this time—May 7, 1945—Robert L. Gilruth became first WFF employee and head of the auxiliary Flight Response Station. His first task was to assemble a staff, and by 1946 he had 40 research engineers working for him, with over half that number coming from Langley. The mission of the flight facility at the time was to establish a Pilotless Aircraft Research Station (PARS) with the duties of checking instruments, installing internal rocket motors and mating them with booster rockets for launching, and testing preflight burners (later called preflight jets). The most significant problem of the time, besides the primitiveness of the island, was transportation. (Image courtesy of Joseph Adam Shortal.)

83

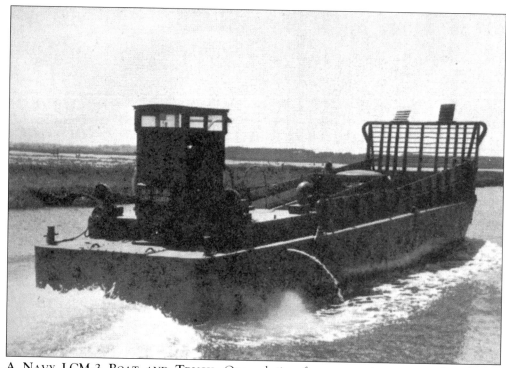

A NAVY LCM-3 BOAT AND TRUCK. One solution for transporting personnel and such equipment as the SCR-584 radar, computers, and plot boards from Langley to Wallops and back was to use two LCM 3-boats on loan from the Navy. Later this was replaced by a ferry. Interestingly, the boats, which had also transported trucks, could be driven right onto the beach from the creek. When the ferry came along, a steel pier was put together. In addition, the Navy had converted a 37-foot plane—adding a cabin—into a personnel boat for Langley-Wallops Island employees. (Courtesy of Joseph Adams Shortal.)

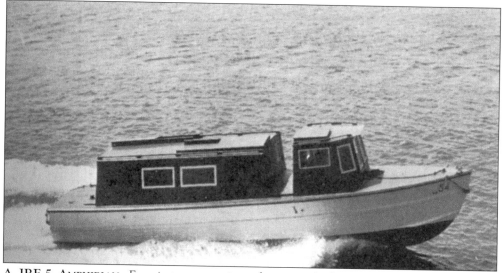

A JRF-5 AMPHIBIAN. For air transportation of personnel, the Navy supplied a Grumman Goose JRF-5 amphibian which greatly aided ground and water landings. (Courtesy of Joseph Adams Shortal.)

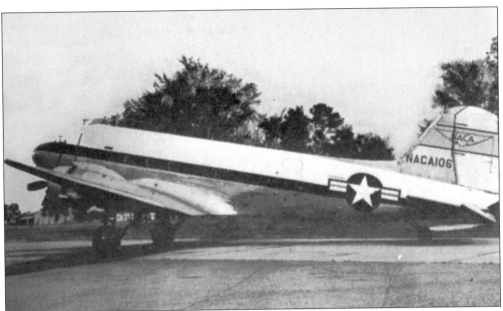

A C47 Airplane. The Army Air Force provided these airplanes for transportation of personnel between Langley and Wallops Island. Being a loan product of NACA, parts were available so repairs weren't problematic. Additionally, Lockheed 12 airplanes were also available, as well as terrain transportation such as a four-wheel drive vehicle (needed because of the lack of paved roads); five jeeps for climbing rough terrain and burrowing through sand; 1/2-ton and 3/4-ton trucks; a 3/4-ton carry-all truck; a 1-1/2-ton cargo truck; a concrete mixer; an air compressor; a welding machine; and perforated steel landing mats. Still, Wallops Island had a long way to go before it could even be referred to as "civilized." (Courtesy of Joseph Adams Shortal.)

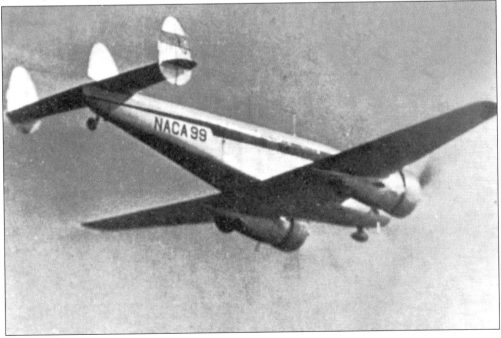

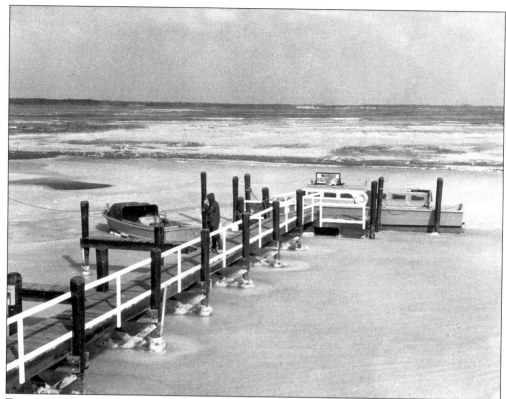

FROZEN SHORELINE. This lone man surveys the ice and snow on the mainland dock. Wallops personnel were transported over to the island by boat. Wallops can be seen in the distance in the middle of the photograph. When the boats were not mobile, if it was necessary, personnel would be flown in. (Photo courtesy of Robert Duffy.)

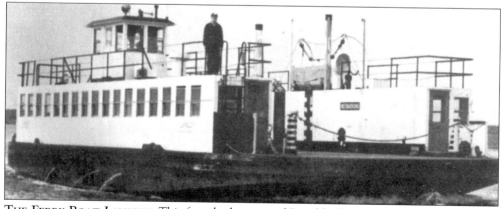

THE FERRY BOAT LANGLEY. This ferry had a crew of 3 and held about 100 passengers. It was used for transportation between the island dock and the mainland. The crossing took about 20 minutes to complete. This was the only means of getting to Wallops Island before the causeway and bridge were built. (Photo courtesy of Joseph Adams Shortal.)

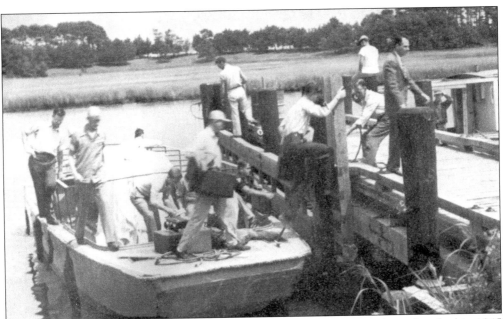

TAYLOR'S LANDING. While Wallops Island was constructing its second wooden shed in 1945 to serve as an office, Taylor's Landing became the first regular departure point on the mainland for water vessels, but because of its shallowness, significant dredging leading from the Landing to Assawoman Creek had to be done. By 1946, the new dock was completed a mile or so downstream, and transportation operations were transferred there. In return for use of Taylor's Landing for deployment of government personnel, NACA dredged Taylor's small boat mooring and turning area. With the mainland dock now dredged out of a creek bank, Langley employees used this main dock to embark and debark. These 1946 photos show the construction of the mainland dock. Notice the graded roads laid leading to the first three stations, though the territory remains barren and primitive. This is where the Grumman Goose Amphibian landed and taxied over the sandy area onto pierced steel mats serving as makeshift ramps. (Courtesy of Joseph Adams Shortal.)

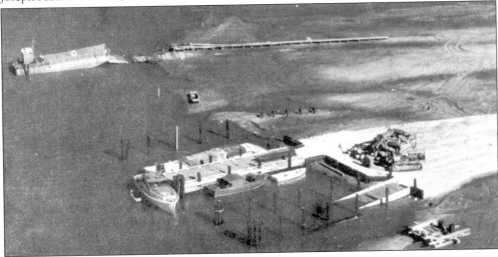

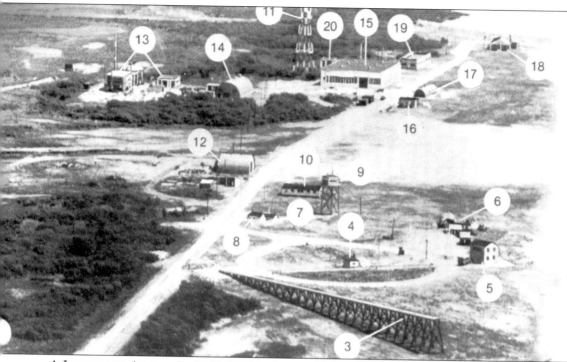

A LANDSCAPE AERIAL. By 1947, WFF had acquired permanent facilities but the base was not included in that year's budget; hence, what is featured here is what had been allocated for 1946 funds: (1) a seawall to protect Wallops Island Shore and buildings from storms (see the close-up on p. 89), requiring the base to purchase $300,000 insurance policy from Lloyds of London; (2) solid fuel storage; (3) launching ramps ($15,000) of 400 feet of wooden ramp and steel rails at a 4-degree slope; (4) an observation shelter; (5) a launching platform ($40,000), as well as two split houses; (6) a temporary instrumentation buildings (7) high pressure buildings; (8) a final loading building; (9) an observation tower (control tower); (10) temporary buildings; (11) a water tower; (12) the fire station; (13) a preflight test unit; (14) the generating plant; (15) the Final Assembly Building Shop ($232,500), at 104-by-158 feet, a combination woodshop and shop; (16) oil tanks for liquid fuel storage; (17) temporary buildings; (18) a utility building; (19) the administration building; and (20) the heating plant. (Courtesy of Joseph Adams Shortal.)

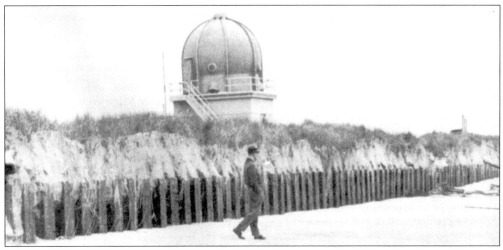

SHORELINE STABILIZATION. Preventing the erosion of the shore was a major problem because of the number of storms that abraded and amassed sand. An intact shoreline was vital to the base in order to continue its launches at the tune of millions of dollars. The goal was to provide a level of protection for the island from Nor'easters, tropical storms, hurricanes, coastal flooding, and erosion. Funding was also allocated for repairing and extending the existing seawall as well as providing beach replenishment from dredging, and through the construction of dunes.

A LIST OF FIRST DEFICIENCY APPROPRIATION. This record emphasizes the projected and final costs of each item listed in the research station. Notice the differences between what was allocated to what was actually spent, some of which cost two and three times the estimates, as seen in the launching site hitch that went over budget by nearly twice as much. The same holds true for what was rationed for utilities. Likewise, $142,000 was allocated for the preflight blower, which in actuality cost almost three times as much at about $400,000. On the other hand, some items came in under the allotted budget, such as the "contingency fund" set at $410,000 when only $3,371 was used. Overall, the appropriations budge balanced out at $4,100,000. (Courtesy of Joseph Adams Shortal.)

TABLE II. DISPOSITION OF 1945 FIRST DEFICIENCY APPROPRIATION

Number on Figure 46	Project Number	Item	May 1945 Estimate	Final Expenditure
	371	Auxiliary Flight Research Station	3,060,000	3,212,002
	A.	Langley Field Station	1,087,300	1,361,996
	1.	Model Shop Extension	(151,000)	(152,581)
	2.	Missile Construction Shop	(485,000)	(781,033)
	3.	Launching Site	(451,300)	(428,382)
	B.	Receiving Station	(105,000)	(22,318)
	C.	Launching Site	892,200	1,622,484
3	1.	Launching Ramp	(15,000)	(39,003)
5	2.	Launching Platform	(10,000)	(1)
15	3.	Final Assembly Building	(232,500)	(195,267)
19	4.	Office and Radio Building	(28,000)	(61,018)
18	5.	Living Quarters	(44,000)	(97,050)
16	6.	Oil Tanks	(20,000)	(29,104)
2	7.	Powder and Chemical Storage	(25,000)	(11,742)
8	8.	Loading Room	(7,500)	(1)
4	9.	Bombproof Shelter	(9,000)	(3,550)
1, 7, 11	10.	Site Purchase or Lease	(20,000)	(401)
14, 20	11.	Utilities	(338,800)	(653,397)
13	12.	Preflight Blower	(142,400)	(400,505)
9	—	Observation Tower	0	(30,000)
12	—	Quonset Hut (Fire Station)	0	(5,500)
6 10, 17	—	Temporary Facilities	0	(51,999)
	—	Equipment	0	(43,948)
	D.	Observation Stations	(9,000)	(1)
	E.	Airplanes	0	0
	F.	Ground Transportation	(6,750)	(2)
	G.	Water Transportation	0	0
	H.	Missiles	(601,200)	0
	I.	Instrumentation	(358,470)	(205,204)
	363	Supersonic Tunnel (Langley)	650,000	884,627
	414	Contingency Fund	410,000	3,371
		Total	4,100,000	4,100,000

Notes: (1) Part of temporary facilities.
(2) Motor vehicles purchased from separate appropriation.

The breakdown of the costs of the different facilities at Wallops, as given in table II, was based on requests sent to NACA Headquarters by Langley, for reallocation of funds, and upon estimates made by Langley engineering personnel. Inasmuch as the Doyle and Russell contract covered practically all the permanent facilities in a lump sum, it was difficult to obtain an accurate breakdown. Most of the facilities were completed and in use by the end of 1946.
Experience at Wallops had shown that under severe storm conditions the ocean came ashore in

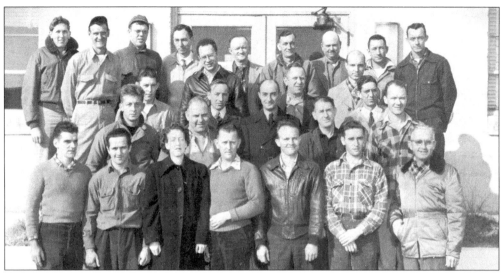

WALLOPS ISLAND PERSONNEL. These two 1950 images feature personnel of the time, which readily changed from year-to-year, depending on the organizational structure as NACA was being converted to NASA. Research personnel remained separate from the administrative employees, not only in job positions, but also in actual working conditions, as seen in something as simple as in transporting men between Wallops and Langley where two boats were used—one for each type of worker. Later, ferries replaced the boats, and school buses were acquired to facilitate the transportation system. Personnel featured in above include the following, from left to right: (front row) D. Watkinson, Shreaves, S. Watkinson, H. Bloxom, Holdren, Daisey, Tyndall, Young, and Reid; (second row) Evans, Watson, Cutler, Merritt, Kellam, and McAllen; (third row) Turlington, W.Bloxom, Willett, Colonna, and White; (fourth row) Mears, Walker, Thorton, Birch, R.Watkinson, L. Watkinson, Pennington, Finney, Rumer, Parks, Melson, Rew, and Grant. The image below includes the following, from left to right: (first row) Quillen, Colonna, Pennington, Johnson, Helton, Mears, and Forbes; (second row) Ferguson, Kellam, Fenner, Robbins, Carey, Levy, Smith, Palmer, and Dereng; (third row) Foster, Townsend, McConnell, Hallett, Spinak, Parks, McComb, Roberson, Menning, Hargis, and Cutler. Many of these names are common to Chincoteague even today, as the descendants continue the tradition of remaining on the island.

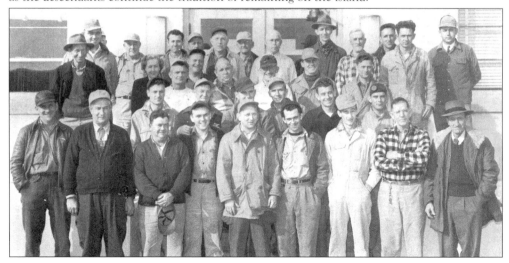

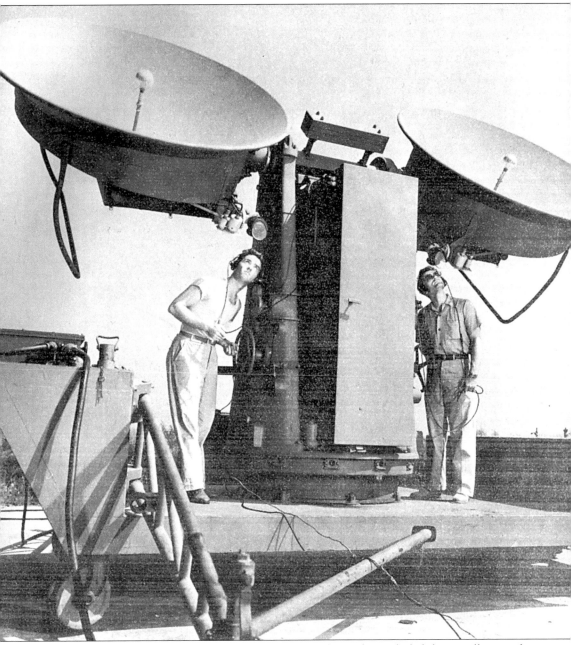

A Velocimeter 10 Radar Doppler. Expansion of facilities also included the installation of instrumentation such as a second SCR-584 radar and a a TPS-5 Doppler Radar, along with a Sperry Model 10 Volocimeter Doppler Radar. Radars were used in every flight launching to collect information on tracking for future use. Once the velocimeter was installed, the Doppler was no longer needed, but this type of sophisticated equipment—for its time—allowed for the execution of weather studies and radiosonde balloons program. Over time, even these instruments became more computerized and high-tech. The men that operated the radar were very brave as they were outside during the launches and not protected by the blockhouse. (Courtesy of Joseph Adams Shortal.)

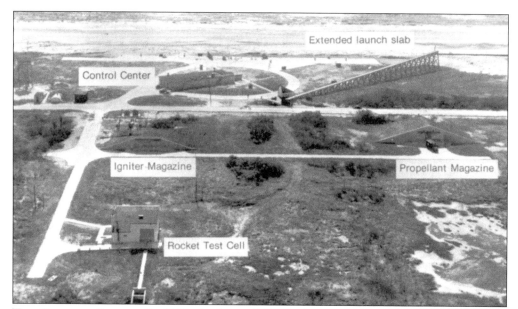

THE CONTROL CENTER. By 1950, the fame of WFF had grown beyond anyone's expectations. Much of this was due to the number of tests being performed and the accuracy in the results of those tests, along with the development of new techniques, and the excitement over the expansion of programs; this, in turn, made more people want to visit the base, although it was still closed to the general public at this time because of "top secret" programs and the concern for safety over hazardous areas. It was during this period that a bombproof instrument station (control center) was built as an annex to the original bombproof observation house control center. The station was 115-by-44-feet, with a floor constructed high enough to be above sea level, made of concrete, with observation ports—all at the cost of $183,750. (Courtesy of Joseph Adams Shortal.)

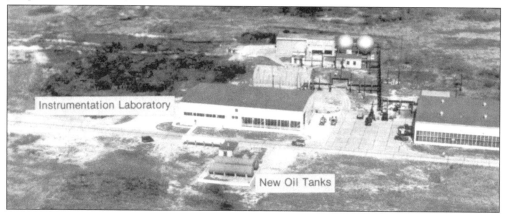

AN AERIAL VIEW OF THE SHOP AREA. This 1950 photo showing the launching area highlights the newly enlarged base, completed in two phases. The first stage yielded a 170-foot extension, carved of 50-foot-wide slab (done in 1948) at the cost of $8,150. The second phase resulted in an extension—in both directions parallel to shoreline—600 feet long by 50 feet wide (89,500); a 37-by-52-foot concrete propellant magazine improvement over small igloos was built in 1945 and 1946; also constructed were an igniter magazine, rocket test cell, instrumentation laboratory (1950), and an expansion of fuel storage capacity. (Courtesy of Joseph Adams Shortal.)

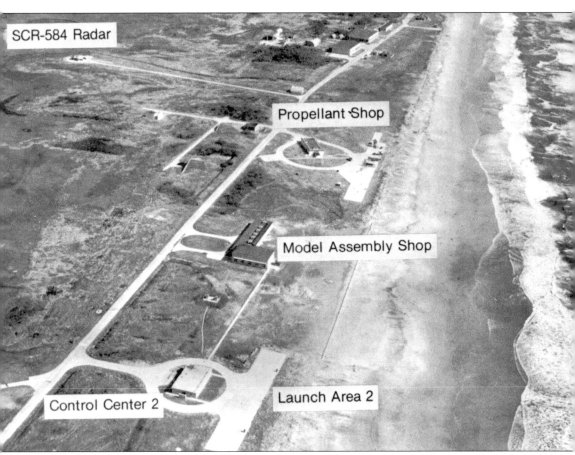

SCR-584 Radar

Propellant Shop

Model Assembly Shop

Control Center 2

Launch Area 2

A NORTH AND SOUTH AERIAL OF WALLOPS ISLAND. Monies that were allocated from the previous year's appropriations allowed Wallops to expand in 1952 through a designed allowance designated at follows: $93,239 for the purchase of the entire island; $315, 915 for the Model Assembly Shop; $166,539 for the Control Center; and $48,672 for the Propellant Shop. Additionally, Stations 1 and 2 cost $12,685; the Ramjet Fuel Storage facility was $12,000; the launch area , as well as the seawall, roads, utilities, and grading, ran about $207,902; and the ferry with its slips was priced around $267,000. Launch Area 2 with its Control Center 2 consisted of a 50-by-300-foot concrete slab running along the ocean front; the Model Assembly Area served as the rocket prep, loading, and storage area; and the Propellant Shop contained these quibs and igniters, with a 13-square-foot boiler room. Included were two camera stations, as well as the construction of additional structures in anticipation of Wallops Station's growth. (Courtesy of Joseph Adams Shortal.)

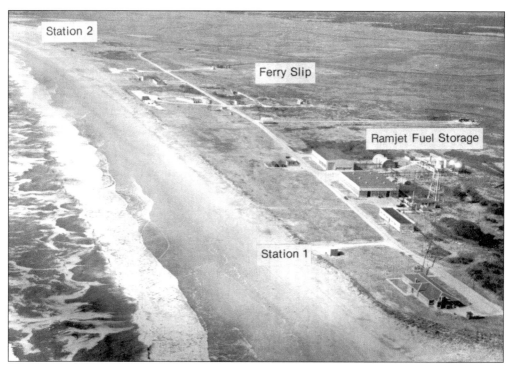

THE RAMJET FUEL STORAGE BUILDING. The building to the far right of the photo illustrates the shape and location of the ramjet fuel storage area, which was 20-by-30 square feet and located near the preflight jet to store its fuel in cylinder-shaped containers. This image also points out the two work stations as well as the costly ferry slip, which replaced both the wartime LCM boats and the two personnel boats, although two smaller boats were kept for emergencies. The ferry, used as transportation between Wallops Island's dock and its mainland dock, could carry people, trucks, and other cargo, and was named the *Langley*. Costing $34,134, it was made of steel construction, 76 feet long, with a beam of 32 feet, and it displaced 109 tons of water with a draft of 5 feet. The boat's wheelhouse was intended to be a one-man operation. The boat channel had to be dredged between the mainland base and the island dock because at low tides, the boats suffered propeller and rudder damage in the marshy, high silt water bottoms. (Courtesy of Joseph Adams Shortal.)

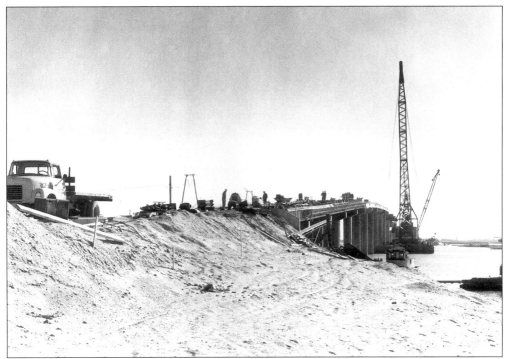

THE CAUSEWAY AND BRIDGE. This photographs depicts the construction of the causeway and bridge from the mainland to Wallops Island. They were opened on March 21, 1960. The bridge, which was constructed by the Tidewater Construction Corporation, has an 80-foot span, 40-foot clearance, and crossed over the mainland waterway. The causeway today (below) is used by a grateful Wallops Island crew. (Photos courtesy of the Spinak family and Bo Bennett.)

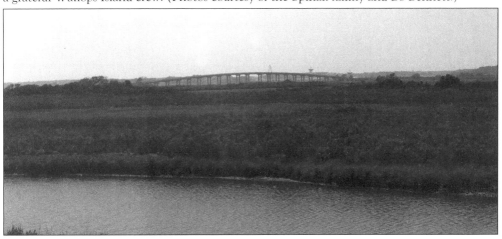

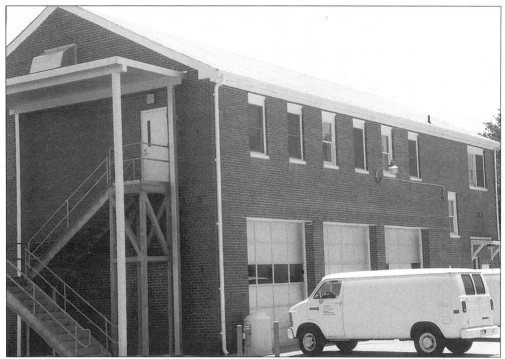

THE OLD FIRE STATION BARRACKS. This old fire station building is now used for building payloads for ultra-long duration balloons. The current balloon program has about 30 yearly missions from the United States and worldwide. Civil servants manage the program and perform the research and development of the balloons. (Photo by Bo Bennett.)

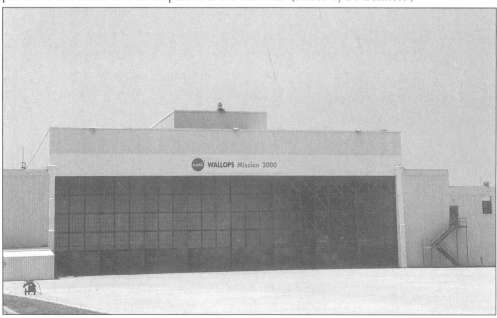

WALLOPS MUSEUM, 2000. This airplane hangar is being refurbished. The Aircraft Projects Office at Wallops operates aircraft to acquire data for airborne science research, providing for a wide variety of experiments. The budget for this project is $4 million. (Photo by Bo Bennett.)

Eight

LIVING CONDITIONS

Living conditions were primitive in 1945. There were no roads or transportation connecting the mainland to other parts of the island, and a ferry or seaplane was needed badly. Wallops Island had no power except for a portable generator, and water had to be ferried in. When Wallops began buying land to build permanent facilities after the war, the state of life improved, but primeval conditions prevailed, so much so that in 1951, because of the crudeness of life, Krieger requested permission to move himself and his family back to Langley. By 1952, the Spartan living conditions were upgraded through the construction of a cafeteria, bunkhouse, and lounge, with bunks costing workers $1 per night. The year 1953 saw cots replacing bunks in the huts, and leather upholstered furniture dotted the lounge, which now boasted a television. In 1960 there was a new round of construction but there was little in the budget for better living conditions. The brightest engineers from international teams arrived on the island to study, and made the hardships all the worse because now there were nearly 300 workers. To show off their engineers and their accomplishments, Wallops Island held its first "open house" in 1968, which still goes on today. During his tenure, Robert Krieger added to Wallops assets by bringing education to the base and the surrounding area.

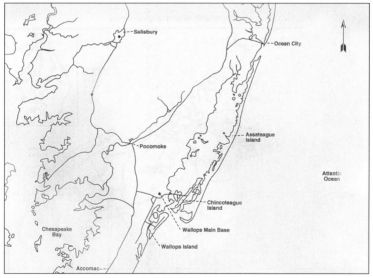

AN AERIAL MAP OF WALLOPS ISLAND, 1945. In 1945, Langley NACA established its launch base on Wallop Islands' southern end. Then, under NACA, the Wallops base moved to the southern end of the island, where there were no trees to limit tracking visibility. This map shows the Hunting Lodge, the NACA Lease Line, the NACA Building (next to the CNAAS), and the relationship of Wallops Island to the town of Chincoteague and the National Reserve of Assateague. (Courtesy of Harold D. Wallace Jr.)

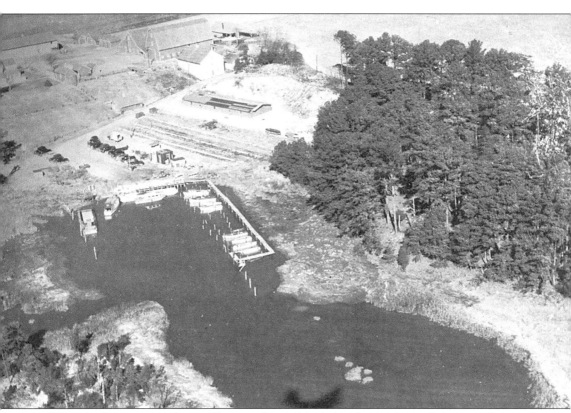

WALLOPS ISLAND AND AREA. The area fostered little besides sand, marsh grass, undergrowth, and sand dunes. NACA had an abundance of unoccupied land to build on, and build it did—starting with the dock area, the launch area, and the work area with living quarters, which were nothing more than temporary shacks, as indicated in this image. Not only was transportation lacking, so were paved roads. Four-wheel vehicles were needed because of the rough and high terrain, along with various types of trucks and various heavy-duty equipment. The first employee—Germaine S. Brown—came from Langley on May 24, 1945, as resident engineer in charge of construction and operations. By 1946, he was joined by 65 men who worked in the pilotless aircraft research programs. (Courtesy of Joseph Adams Shortal.)

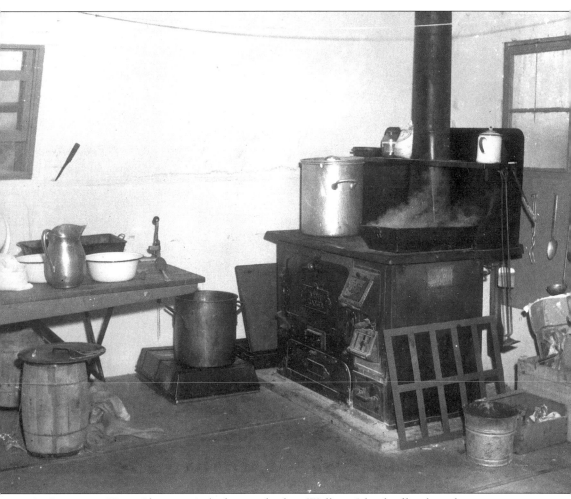

A QUONSET HUT. If it wasn't bad enough that Wallops Island offered, at best, a sparse existence with its lack of transportation, amenities, recreation, and basic necessities, then the living quarters for those staying on the island had to be the lowest of the low points; however, the engineers endured with their focus on research rather than down pillows and fluffy comforters. This image demonstrates the rudimentary nature of the island, as seen in the interior of one of the two Quonset huts serving as living quarters. Here we see the kitchen wing of the "Quonset hut Hotel" as it existed in August 1945. Notice the jury-rigged stove, wooden table and crates, barrels to hold nonperishable foods, and tin pots. In addition to the two huts on the island, there were also six munition storage igloos, five wooden shacks, one operations office, an assembly shed, a general warehouse shed, a radio dispensary, one dark room, and a power generator house. Communication was only accessible via the Coast Guard lines on the land, while links to Langley were limited to radio. (Courtesy of Harold D. Wallace Jr.)

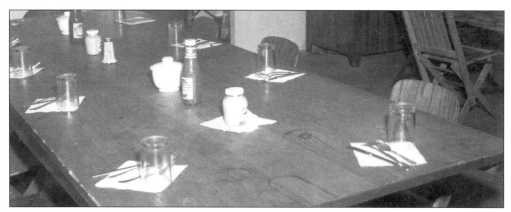

THREE HUTS. In this 1945 collection of photos, we see Quonset huts, which are made of corrugated steel, shaped like a half cylinders. Although they may range in size, standard dimensions are about 50-to-100-feet long, and 20-by-40-feet wide, with the flat part serving as the floor. The name came from the town of Quonset, Rhode Island, which made the first hut for the Navy in 1941. Housing of any type was needed because of crowded sleeping conditions. These huts show the sparseness of the living conditions. They do, however, have a bottle of ketchup on the two dining tables, with salt and pepper and glass vessels. Notice the pantry area in the back. In the exterior view, the hut looks like a can sliced in half with a couple of windows and a regular solid door with a screen door. The sleeping quarters show a minimum of six cots, a few with items thrown over them, aligned in barracks or dorm-style. (Courtesy of Joseph Adams Shortal.)

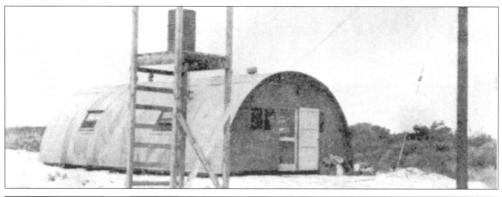

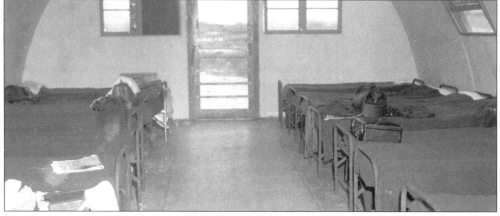

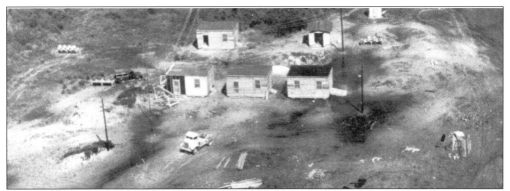

TEMPORARY SHACKS. The word "shack" is an appropriate noun for this type of quarters. If Wallops personnel weren't in Quonset huts, then they were housed in these temporary shacks The Quonset huts were located near the launch area and power lines. They also had drums for oil storage and four gasoline storage tanks. Bathroom facilities consisted of latrines, primitive at best. Tents were the first type housing prior to the arrival of the shacks and the huts. (Courtesy of Joseph Adams Shortal and Harold D. Wallace Jr.)

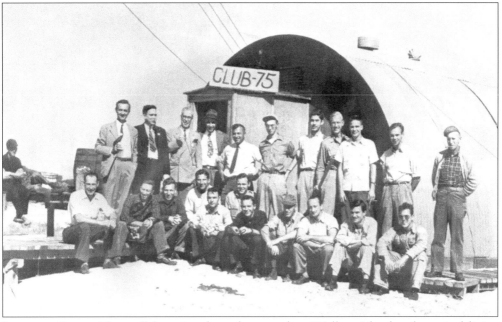

LANGLEY STAFF. The staff from Langley, who served on Wallops Island and required living quarters while there, gather in front of this Quonset hut labeled "Club-75." The Langley employees at Wallops Island had to pay for their food as well as the use of the huts, which cost them about $6 a day. On top of this, they had to deal with terrible and abundant insects that caused a great loss of work time and several resignations. Workers had to brush and shake out their clothes every morning and night to ride them of insects. DDT was sprayed in spite of about 200 ponies living on the island. Back then, DDT was believed to be dangerous only to birds, fish, and oysters, but many of the ponies did get moved to Assateague Island. Pictured in this August 1945 photo of Langley flight operators are the following, from left to right: (front row) Baynes, Seacord, Stoller, Alexander, Plotz, Tracy, Everett, Lundstrom, Pitkin, Garner, and Cavallo; (back row) Stack, Abbott, Reid, Gilruth, Hooker, Fuhrmeister, Taylor, Haynes, Gardiner, and Norfolk. (Courtesy of Joseph Adams Shortal.)

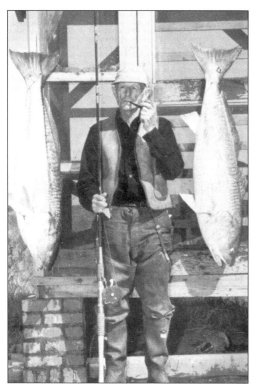

SHERWOOD MORTHAM. In this picture of a classic "islander" with high boots, fishing jacket, and hat, with pipe in one hand and rod in the other, Mortham Stands between two huge catches hanging from a crossbar. Mortham was a night mechanic who lived in the cafeteria building and was responsible for getting the preflight jet pressurized for the next day's testing. Though when not working for Wallops, he spent much time fishing and caught large channel bass in the surf. (Courtesy of Joseph Adams Shortal.)

ISLAND WORK. This 1946 picture shows workers setting up the equipment on the island for upcoming launches. Notice the primitiveness of the work facilities. If accidents occurred, the injured ended up at Salisbury's hospital, about 40 minutes away by car. With the lack of available vehicles on the island, as well as regular roads, the transport of the injured often took longer at the risk of life or limb. (Courtesy of Abe Spinak's family.)

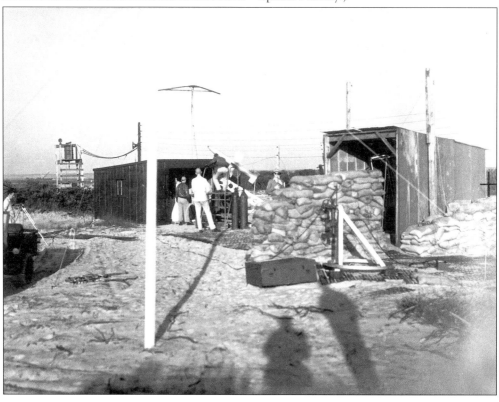

KRIEGER DOCUMENT. This document relates the "mass change" that was to come into effect January 17, 1960, which transferred some of the first main employees to Wallops Island from various stations within NASA. (Courtesy of Robert Krieger's family.)

NATIONAL AERONAUTICS AND SPACE ADMINISTRATION
Wallops Station
Wallops Island, Virginia

January 15, 1960

MASS CHANGE

Reference: NASA Headquarters letter of December 21, 1959
from Director of Business Administration

This is an official notice of personnel action for a change of appointing officer and organizational reassignment effective January 17, 1960.

Your appointment, position, grade and salary are not affected by this change.

From	To
Langley Research Center	Wallops Station
Pilotless Aircraft Research Station	Office of the Chief
Langley Field, Virginia	

—KRIEGER, Robert L.	DOB 8-17-16
DUNN, Roy F.	DOB 3-4-06
WATSON, Cynthia M.	DOB 9-12-26

Joseph E. Robbins
Administrative Officer

GAM:mas

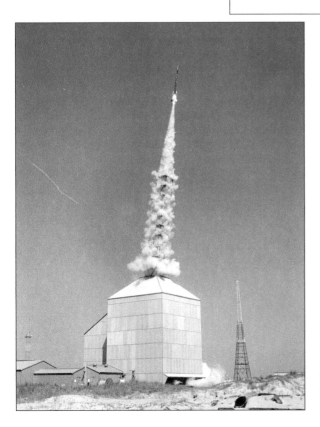

A LAUNCH. One of the first launches from Wallops Island, this rocket can be seen successfully climbing into the sky. The building that is shown here is no longer on the island. (Photo courtesy of Robert Duffy.)

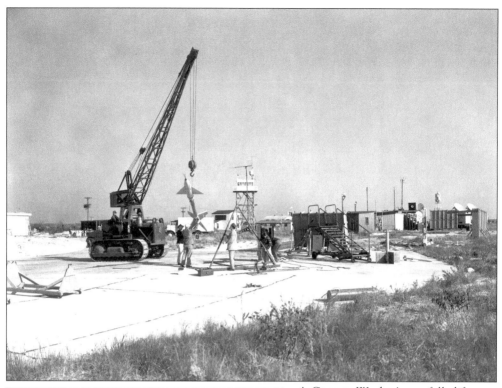

A Crane. Worker's carefully lift a rocket into position. By 1948, the area was full of employees that were kept busy at their assigned jobs from waking to bedtime, and many of them doubled at other jobs. In their limited free time, they swam on the sandy beach directly before breakfast or dinner, as afternoons were devoted to research testing, as seen in this photo. (Courtesy of Abe Spinak's family.)

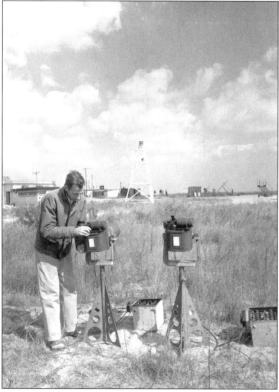

Photography. This engineer sets up his cameras in anticipation of a launch. Battery packs can be seen on the ground next to the cameras. (Courtesy of Abe Spinak's family.)

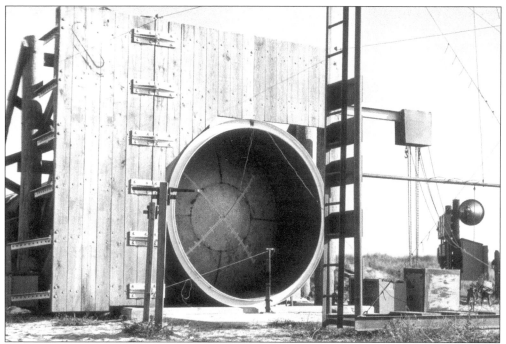

WIND TUNNELS. These tunnels were used as part of the Blast Effects Program. The aircraft models were put in place in front of the shock tube and an explosive charge would be ignited on the inside to test the effects of explosive blasts on the lift of aircraft. They were developing techniques to knock airplanes out of the sky. These blasts would set off a tremendous shock waves. The men would stand about 1,500 feet down from the tunnels. In 1958, Robert Duffy came back to the island after being on a different assignment for a year. After his first blast, Duffy walked over to the instrument shack. When he looked inside, a man stumbled and dropped to the floor. Duffy started toward the man, who then rolled over and smiled, saying "Welcome back to Wallops." Imagine living next to these tunnels! (Photos courtesy of the Spinak family.)

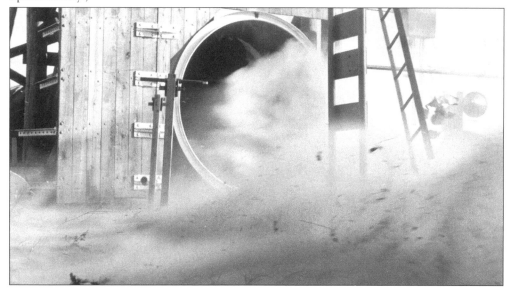

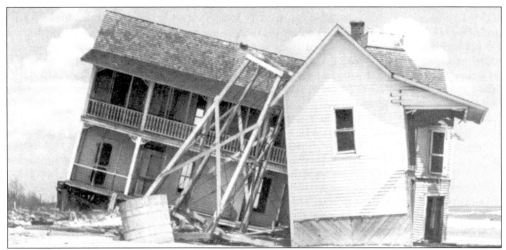

CLUBHOUSE EROSION. This May 1949 picture portrays the decay of the Wallops Island Association clubhouse, which at one time had served as a fishing and hunting lodge for well-heeled northerners and urbanites, some of whom resided in Philadelphia. The association sold the lodge and land at the insistence of the federal government for the use of NACA/NASA, who allowed it to fall in disrepair. Shortal offers, "The clubhouse . . . was abandoned and became the victim of beach erosion, winds, high water, and waves. . . . Although local residents . . . would have welcomed the opportunity to use [it] and the beach . . . both the Navy and NACA . . . restrict[ed] the island to official use," although employees did use it for picnics. (Courtesy of Joseph Adams Shortal.)

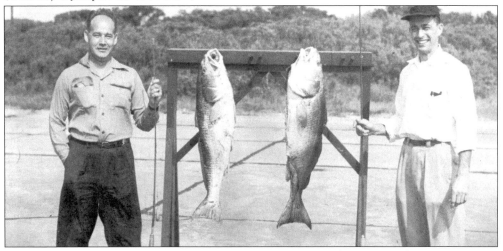

KRIEGER FISHING. By 1953 Wallops was sporting a lunchroom/cafeteria, lodging now costing only $1 per day, a lounge, and various recreational activities such as horseshoes. In this image, Robert Krieger is pictured with his catch of the day with fellow employee E.D. Schult. The channel bass or drum fish were caught off Wallops Island Beach. Angling was another form of recreation because the island had an abundance of fish throughout the year. Fishing or surf casting was done by the employees and transient visitors who brought their own rod and reel. Spring offered the channel bass and drum fish, as seen in this May picture, weighing 35 to 50 pounds. Lightweight fishermen had to sit on the beach and dig their heels into sand to prevent themselves from being sucked into the ocean by large fish in the area. (Courtesy of Joseph Adams Shortal.)

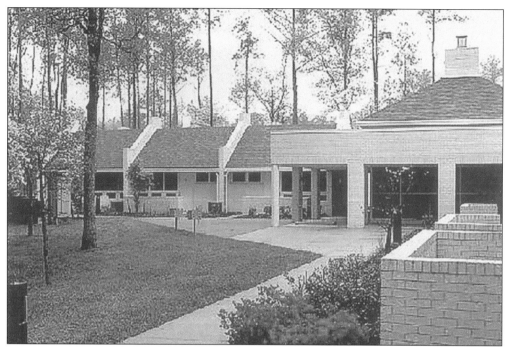

BACHELOR QUARTERS. These present quarters are for single Naval officers, as this branch (AEGIS) of the military shares Wallops Island with the flight station. Sixteen rooms are available including a kitchenette, a small living room, and a bedroom. Compare these modern conveniences to the Quonset huts of some 50 years earlier. (Courtesy of AEGIS.)

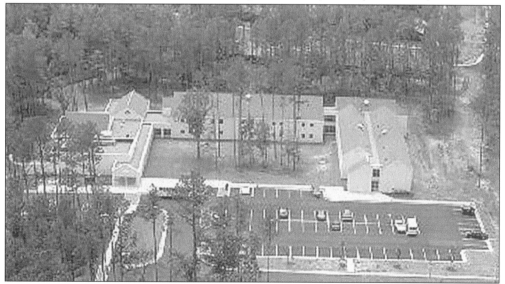

NAVY HOUSING. This housing complex is for enlisted men and women who do not have families. The complex includes a pool table, cafeteria, laundry room, and a barber shop. In this aerial view, the differences can be seen between the officer quarters at the top of the page and the dormitory, project-styled accommodations featured here. Although the military maintains a presence on the island, much of the base's work is done by civilians today. (Courtesy of AEGIS.)

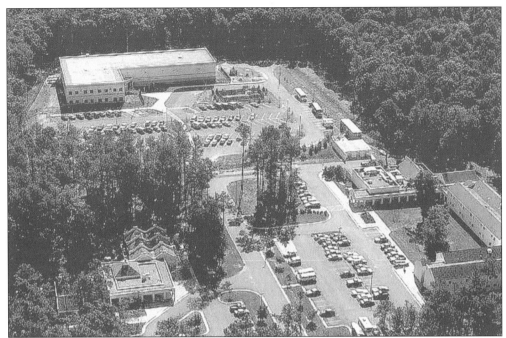

THE SURFACE COMBAT SYSTEMS CENTER (SCSC). Just as AEGIS partners with Wallops Flight Facility, SCSC is also a tenant. This aerial view depicts a large building nestled in the trees in the background containing the systems' headquarters, while the bachelor quarters with its dining area is located in the left forefront. The structure at the right is for Navy enlistees and families. SCSC and all its buildings are located on the mainland outside of Wallops Flight Facility, west of Chincoteague. SCSC's coast site is situated on the island about 10 miles south of these headquarters. (Courtesy of AEGIS.)

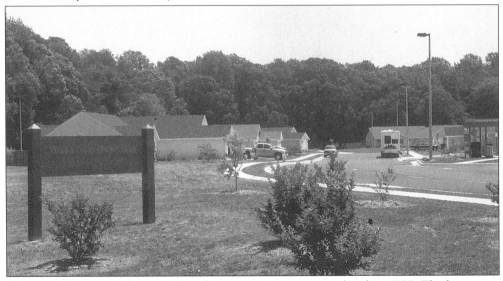

WALLOPS HOUSING. This new Navy housing project was completed in 1999. The homes are available in two and three bedrooms. A playground is available and a pool may be added in the future as well as additional housing for the Coast Guard. Land is available for further development in the future if another phase is built for the Navy. (Photo by Bo Bennett.)

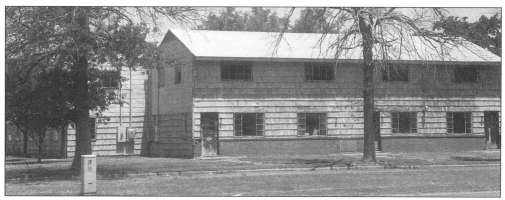

THE MARINE SCIENCE CONSORTIUM (MSC). Today college students from around the country stay in these dormitories to participate in the Marine Science Project Consortium, which is comprised of various educational institutions. The buildings, constructed originally as housing for Navy personnel during World War II, were converted in 1964 for use as a branch of the University of Virginia, which Krieger was instrumental in bringing about. It continued in this capacity on Wallops Island until July 1, 1971, when it merged with Virginia's Community College system and was renamed the Eastern Shore Community College. Three years later, the campus moved from the island to its current site in Melfa, Virginia, where it boasts new and modern structures and programs. The building pictured here is one of the few no longer in use; other such quarters have been remodeled and transformed into MSC dormitories, classrooms, and labs. (Photo by Bo Bennett.)

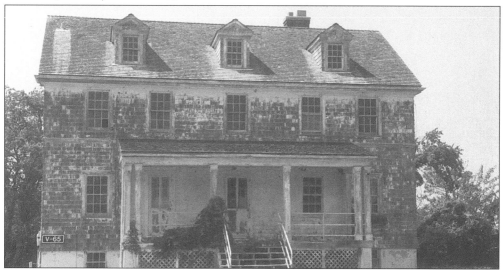

THE COAST GUARD FACILITY. This old structure served as home to the Coast Guard back in the 1930s, when power was obtained through generators and living facilities were even more prehistoric than those of NACA's Wallops in the mid-1940s. However, the Coast Guard is remembered for their goodwill and charity to the local teenage boys. Emmet Taylor fondly remembers a Coast Guard crew offering sandwiches to the hungry teens who would hitch a ride on a monitor that was in the area and walk across the marsh, then over to the beach to get to the ocean. The beach was quite wide back in the 1930s, but over time the ocean has eroded both the dunes and this structure, though in its early days it served the military and locals well. Not only did Taylor's family and friends enjoy having picnics on Wallops' north end, but the south end was equally coveted. (Photo by Bo Bennett.)

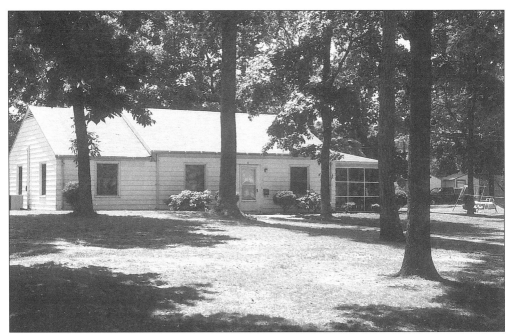

WORLD WAR II HOUSING. This home was originally located on the Wallops Island base and was offered as housing for World War II servicemen. It since has been moved outside of the base to Mill Pond Road and now serves as living quarters for families of the Coast Guard. The clean-looking siding, wide windows, and a porch off to the right give it the appearance of a home that could belong to any civilian anywhere. In comparing this building to the projects in previous pages, we can see that the military has come a long way in providing their personnel with better, modern, and clean-looking homes. (Photo by Bo Bennett.)

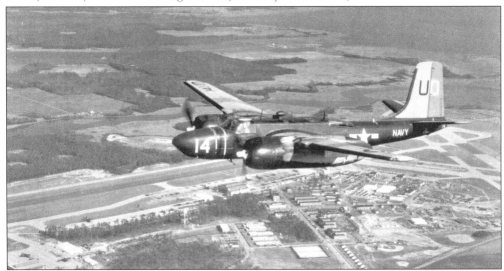

A WORLD WAR II NAVY PLANE. This aerial photo not only features a Navy military plane but it also shows the nature of housing on the Wallops Island base during World War II. Note how the homes are lined up at the bottom left foreground as though they were bowling pins. Over the years, many of these accommodations were transformed into "projects" for civilians who needed starter homes or low-rent apartment facilities. (Photo by Bo Bennett.)

Nine

SECURITY AND SAFETY

Disasters proved problematic during the period when WFF was considered top security—no one was allowed to visit the island without prior authorization to protect classified information from saboteurs. But even the best security can be breeched, as in 1952 ,when two Wallops Island guards were surprised by a boat that came ashore at 1:30 a.m. Immediately, authorities assumed it was an enemy vessel, when in reality it was a sea trawler manned by a Captain Swann, from Atlantic City, New Jersey, who thought the Wallops lights were those of the Chincoteague Inlet. Both the guards and Swann were surprised to see each other when coming face-to-face. This, in turn, made WFF top brass all the more neurotic about security threats, along with safety measures to protect workers and visitors from explosions, rocket crashes, contamination, fires, and other potential catastrophes. Despite the planning and foresight of administrators, WFF wasn't immune from security breaks and accidents. What follows is an overview of some of the problems faced by WFF.

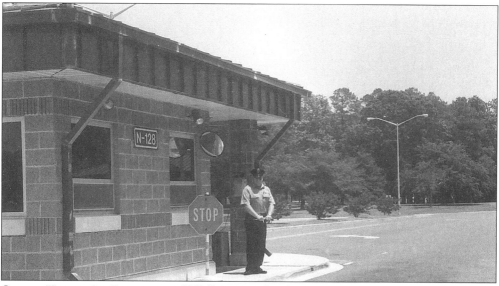

GUARD HOUSE. Joe Porter, one of Wallops' guards, pleasantly greets people as they arrive on the base. The guards ascertain whether patrons are there for work or official business. Anyone entering the base or Wallops Island must have a pass or an I.D. badge. If a person is visiting the base or the island, the guard will direct them to Security Headquarters to have a temporary pass issued. I.D.'s are checked and phone calls are made before entering either property. Once cleared, a badge must be worn wear so it is visible on your clothing at all times. Upon departure, the badges are turned in at the gatehouse. Also, all employees of any entity on the facility must have a profile/background check done prior to being hired.

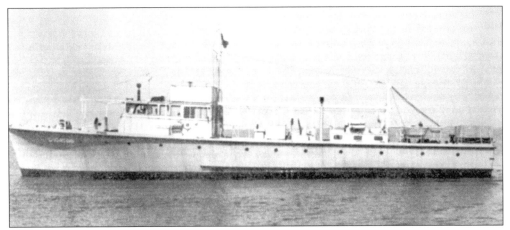

A RESCUE BOAT. Transportation between Langley and Wallops Island presented itself as a major problem, requiring many legs to get from one base to the other. For example, a C-47 first had to fly personnel to NASA, then truck or sail everyone to WFF. The boat ride—if weather permitted—from Langley required two hours of sailing time; railroad transportation took four hours; the Norfolk Little Creek Ferry, which ran every two hours, took six to eight hours; and the Cape Charles boat only ran twice a day. WFF finally received a 104-foot-long rescue boat from the Navy on July 11, 1945, that could carry people and cargo in nearly all types of weather, except extremely severe and rough weather. The vessel let Langley employees make the trip to and from Wallops Island in one day. It remained in operation until 1955. However, before any boat could arrive at WFF's dock, the channel had to be dredged because it had filled with silt and at low tide caused propeller damage. Beacons and reflectors were also installed to mark the waterway. (Courtesy of Joseph Adams Shortal.)

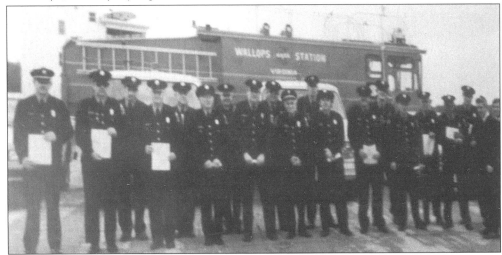

EARLY 80S. These 20 firemen pose in front of the old Wallops Station fire truck on the eastern shore of Virginia at WFF. The firemen were responsible for conducting and maintaining a fire inspection on all buildings on the base as well as on the island and offer fire protection and rescue for all Navy and NASA employees. One difference between the firemen then and now are the training scenarios, which used to include an actual jet fuel fire. This would be put out with a 1.5-inch hose. Today the firemen use at least a 1.75-inch hose because it allows a greater volume of water and higher flow rate if necessary, and jet fuel is no longer used. (Photo courtesy of NASA and Wallops Flight Facility.)

A Deacon Booster. On August 2, 1951, a Deacon booster motor accidentally fired. This was the most serious accident to occur at Wallops Island. Durwood A. Dereng, a technician, performed his usual job of checking for flight readiness. The MX-775B Northrop Boojum missile was being prepared for take off (right) and Dereng received the control tower's message that all systems were ready to switch from external to internal power. When he turned the switch to the internal power, he pulled the plug, causing the telemeter to stop operating. Dereng then put the plug back in, upon directions from the control tower, and proceeded to turn the switch on and off several times. Within seconds, the motor fired, severely cracking his left hand while a booster fin nearly severed his right hand. He was rushed to a mainland dock by a speed boat and taken to the hospital by ambulance, where his hand beyond his wrist was amputated. This accident caused changes in procedure to be implemented, one of which was the external plug was pulled from a safe distance. The photo below portrays Dereng back at work at WFF mastering the use of his artificial hand. Dereng also would sit in on safety seminars while the new personnel were being told how important it was to follow all safety measures. (Courtesy of Joseph Adams Shortal.)

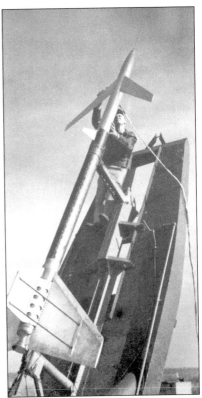

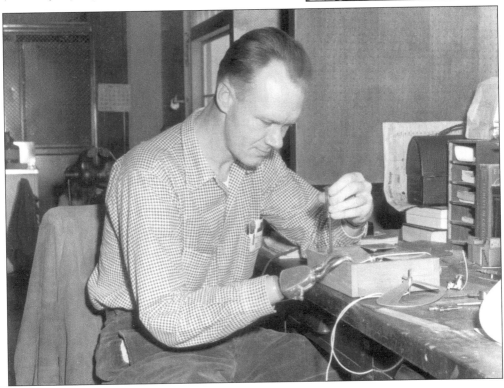

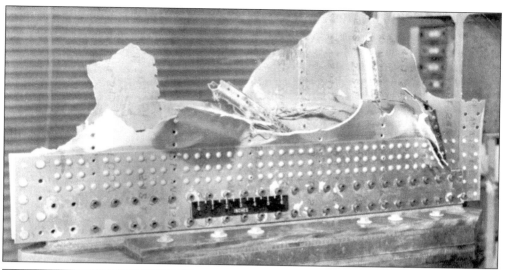

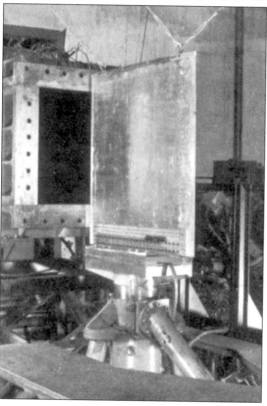

RESEARCH WING REMAINS. If a rocket's wings don't hold up to wind resistance and high temperature, a cataclysmic accident will occur, killing everyone aboard in manned flights. Hence, rocket wing structures were exposed to a variety of stress testing, as seen in these two 1952 images. The image at left shows a 40-inch chord and span in a 27-inch Mach 2 nozzle of WFF's preflight jet; the test was designed to gather information on temperature distribution over the wing span. The wing's exposure to the jet went fine for the first 7.5 seconds, and then it abruptly began vibrating, and the model was destroyed within 2 seconds, surprising all the engineers. Above is an image of the 40-inch-wing span structure after failing the test, indicating the melting and crinkling of the material. Imagine the effect of this had this been an actual manned flight. (Courtesy of Joseph Adams Shortal.)

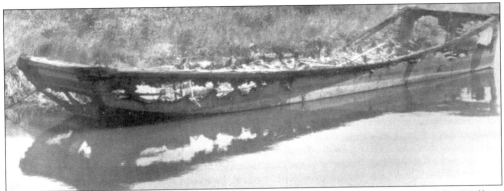

A DAMAGED PERSONNEL BOAT. On July 1, 1953, a gasoline fire erupted on one of the Wallops personnel boats as it was loading passengers at the mainland dock. The boat had been converted from a Navy barge into a carrier of mechanical and administrative employees, but on this occasion, the carrier had aboard administrators when the explosion catapulted five people from the deck. Of the 13 men aboard, the four in the cabin below by the rear door escaped serious injury; the other nine who were seated closest to the engine received first and second-degree burns, leaving many scarred for life. The men were taken to the Chincoteague Naval Air Station Hospital for immediate care. (Courtesy of Joseph Adams Shortal.)

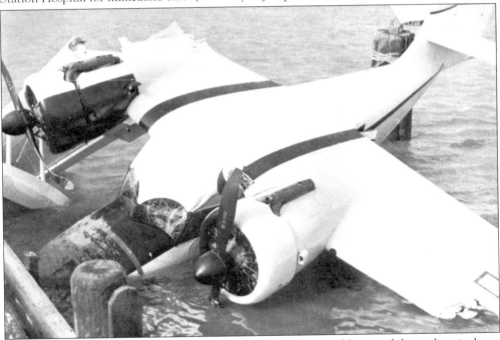

THE WRECK OF AN AMPHIBIAN PLANE. Not only were there problems with boats, but airplanes were also subject to catastrophes. Although this accident was minor, resulting in no serious injuries, it reminded personnel at WFF that the isolated island wasn't shielded from disasters. In this photo, a Grumman JRF-5 amphibian plane crashed into the Wallops Island dock during a landing run on November 3, 1954. This accident was due to a strong gust of wind that veered the plane off course; the weather contributed greatly to the success of navigating an amphibian, as did the number of riders and the nature of cargo. This plane was extensively damaged but all the passengers safely evacuated (albeit some bruises and abrasions) through the door and over the wing to the dock. (Courtesy of Joseph Adams Shortal.)

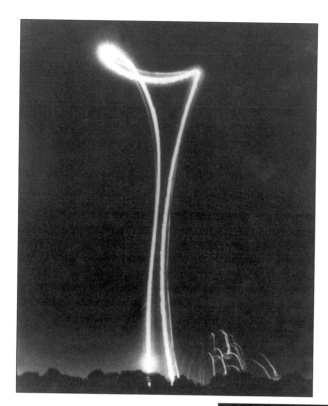

A Rocket Blowing Up. This Scout malfunctioned, immediately returning to the ground only seconds after it was launched into the night. Spectators (below) watch from the grandstand. (Photo courtesy of Robert Duffy.)

The Grand Stand. Spectators safely witnessed launches from the grandstand on the mainland. On the night of the mishap shown above, Robert Duffy's mother and aunt were present along with his wife and one of her friends. As the younger ladies realized the launch had malfunctioned, they rapidly left the stand. It is reported the Duffy's mother stared after them, stayed right where she was, and turned to her sister saying "If it were not safe for us to be here Bob would have said so." Mrs. Duffy remained right where she was, having absolute faith in her son. (Photo courtesy of Robert Duffy.)

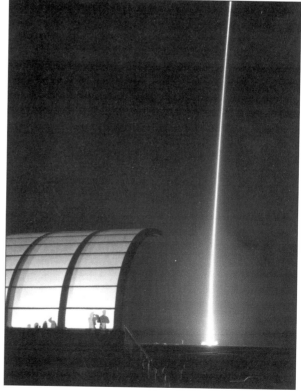

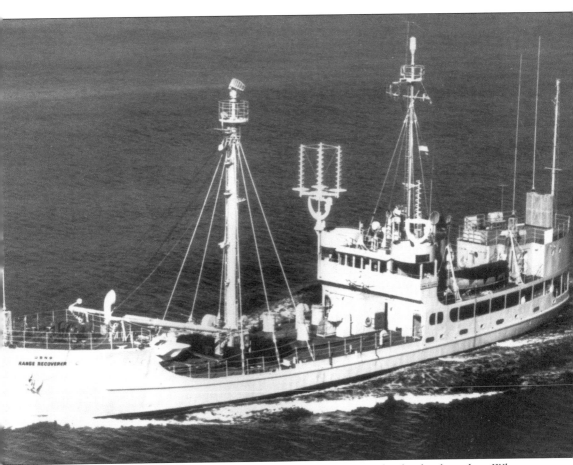

THE RANGE RECOVER. The *Range Recover* was used to recover payloads after launches. When rockets are launched the ship can ascertain the rocket's position with the equipment they have on board. The ship was also utilized for other missions, including being sent to Greece to collect scientific data during the eclipse. (Photo courtesy of NASA and Wallops Flight Facility.)

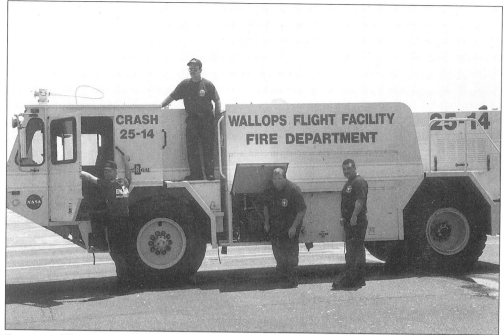

FIREMEN. These men stand with their brand new fire truck that came over from Virginia Langley Airport. Shown here from left to right are Timmy McCready, Dave Kulley, Bryan Daffin, and Bobby Lappin. Today there are 27 full-time firefighters who offer support with emergency medical services outside of the base if they are needed, from Salisbury, Maryland, to Onely, Virginia. If NASA requires assistance in another state, the men will fly anywhere they are needed. On the base and island they perform fire protection for all Navy and NASA buildings. In addition, they offer fire protection and rescue for all NASA, military, and experimental aircraft that use the airport, and perform hazardous material clean-up and contamination prevention. (Photo courtesy of NASA and Wallops Flight Facility.)

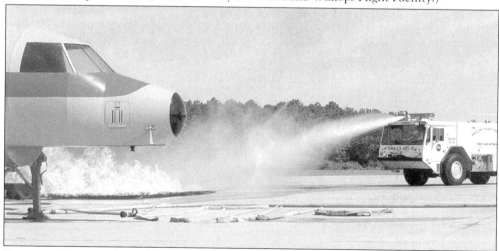

PRACTICE. Firemen shown here are practicing for an actual fuel fire, if one should ever occur. They simulate this scenario in the big box on the ground. A diesel fuel gas mixture is set on fire and then quickly put out in a matter of seconds with water and foam. (Photo courtesy of NASA and Wallops Flight Facility.)

Ten

THE FUTURE

In the year 2000, Wallops Flight Facility continues to function as a generalized multi-facet research center, providing the low-cost integration, launch, and operation of suborbital and small orbital payloads and furthering scientific, educational, and economic advancement. Studies of earth science and global change will also move forward. The management of NASA's Balloon Program and Ultra Long Duration Balloon Project as well as the Small Shuttle Payload Projects, SPARTAN, SPARTAN Lite, and the Hitchhiker series, will continue to grow. Other undertakings include the Sounding Rockets Program, the Orbital Tracking Program, and the operation of scientific aircraft, Wallops' launch range, and its research airport.

Wallops has an open house every five years in the summer months beginning 9:00 a.m., rain or shine. The next open house will be held in 2005. The event generally includes tours of NASA, Navy, NOAA, and the U.S. Coast Guard. Food is available as well as music, a children's tent, entertainment featuring the U.S. Navy Band, and demonstrations (such as model rockets).

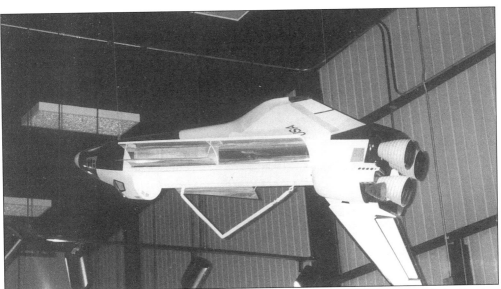

A SHUTTLE MODEL. This space shuttle model can be seen at the Wallops Flight Facility Visitors Center. The space shuttle has been flying for two decades and October 2000 will mark its 100th flight. The shuttle has been the cornerstone of the USA space program and is the world's only reusable space craft. It is the first vehicle in the history of space flight that can carry large cargos such as satellites and space station parts both to and from orbit. (Photo by Bo Bennett.)

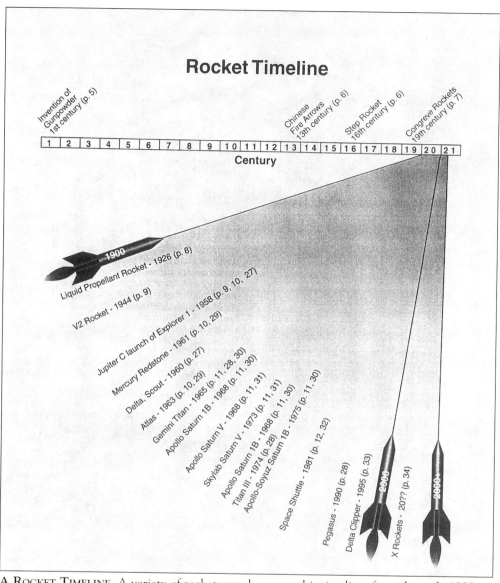

Rocket Timeline

Invention of Gunpowder 1st century (p. 5)

Chinese Fire Arrows 13th century (p. 6)

Step Rocket 16th century (p. 6)

Congreve Rockets 19th century (p. 7)

| 1 | 2 | 3 | 4 | 5 | 6 | 7 | 8 | 9 | 10 | 11 | 12 | 13 | 14 | 15 | 16 | 17 | 18 | 19 | 20 | 21 |

Century

1900

Liquid Propellant Rocket - 1926 (p. 8)

V2 Rocket - 1944 (p. 9)

Jupiter C launch of Explorer 1 - 1958 (p. 9, 10, 27)

Mercury Redstone - 1961 (p. 10, 29)

Delta, Scout - 1960 (p. 27)

Atlas - 1963 (p. 10, 29)

Gemini Titan - 1965 (p. 11, 28, 30)

Apollo Saturn 1B - 1968 (p. 11, 30)

Apollo Saturn V - 1968 (p. 11, 31)

Skylab Saturn 1B - 1973 (p. 11, 31)

Apollo Saturn 1B - 1968 (p. 11, 31)

Titan III - 1974 (p. 28)

Apollo-Soyuz Saturn 1B - 1975 (p. 11, 30)

Space Shuttle - 1981 (p. 12, 32)

Pegasus - 1990 (p. 28)

Delta Clipper - 1995 (p. 33)

X Rockets - 20?? (p. 34)

2000

2001

A ROCKET TIMELINE. A variety of rockets are shown on this timeline, from the early 1900s to 2001, with the latest in rocket technology being the x-rockets, which are being researched and tested today at the Marshall Space Flight Center in the Alabama Jet Propulsion Laboratory. In 1926 liquid fuelled rockets were used, which led to the x-rockets of today. (Photo courtesy of NASA and Wallops Flight Facility Education Center.)

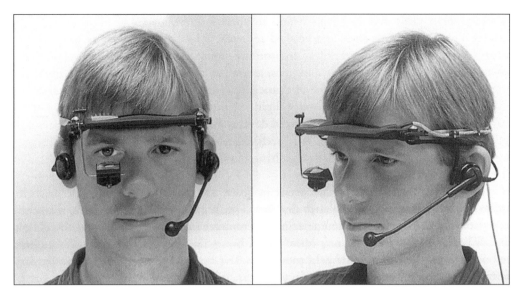

INTERNATIONAL SPACE STATION TECHNOLOGY. The small headset this person is modeling shows the technology that can be used within the space station to allow the astronauts to receive up-to-date visual and audio data anywhere on the station. These operate on a two-way wireless link so the astronauts can keep in constant contact with each other. The headsets are lightweight and easily transported, and will benefit safety, health, and productivity in space and on earth. (Photo courtesy of NASA and Wallops Flight Facility.)

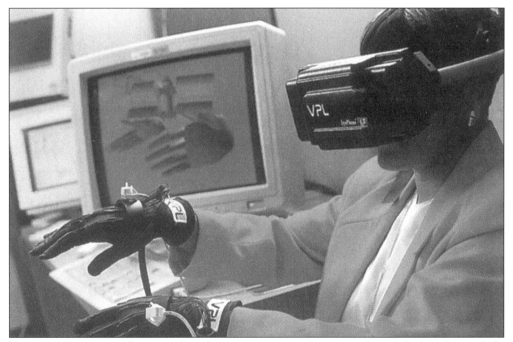

VIRTUAL REALITY. This virtual reality experiment is being conducted by NASA to help further education by being able to simulate real life situations in the medical field (virtual person), as well as having astronauts train as though they are on the International Space Station. (Photo courtesy of NASA and Wallops Flight Facility.)

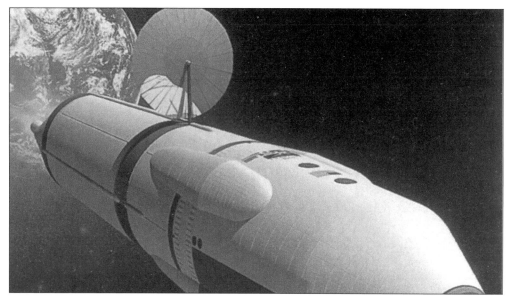

A FUTURE SPACE VEHICLE. The planned missions for the astronauts on the International Space Station will require long periods of space travel. These space vehicles will need to sustain the astronauts for months and even years without receiving any additional supplies from earth. Many studies are being done to develop advanced life support systems and recycling procedures. (Photo courtesy of NASA and Wallops Flight Facility.)

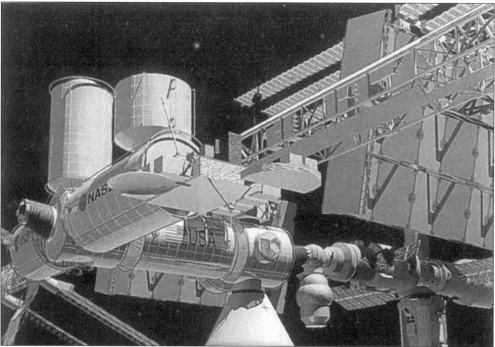

THE SPACE STATION. The ISS will be used in the future to test and validate systems that will be intended for use on far reaching missions. Pictured here is the Mars habitat testbed that is being tested for a future mission for human habitability and being able to withstand some of the harsh space environments. (Photo courtesy of NASA and Wallops Flight Facility.)

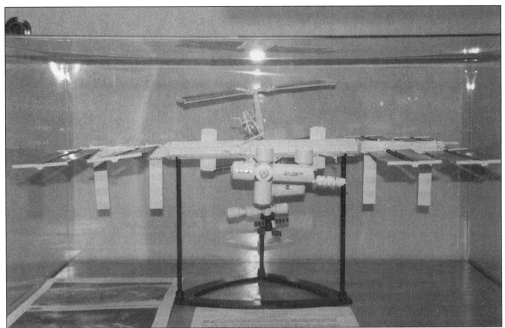

THE ISS. The prototype of the International Space Station is pictured here as it is found in the foyer of the Wallops Flight Facility F-6 Building. Although the space station is not fully constructed it is habitable. It is currently being used for zero gravity research and is the stage for future space missions. These missions will leave from the space station to their next destination. Hopefully, soon a mission to Mars will begin from the station. Tests are being conducted to develop a safe mission environment. A variety of nations and organizations are participating in the ISS project, including the European space agency, Canadian space agency, and Japan. The station is 13 stories tall and is only equipped at this time with one bathroom. (Photo by Bo Bennett.)

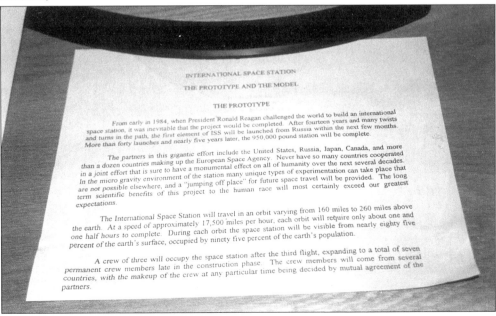

INTERNATIONAL SPACE STATION

THE PROTOTYPE AND THE MODEL

THE PROTOTYPE

From early in 1984, when President Ronald Reagan challenged the world to build an international space station, it was inevitable that the project would be completed. After fourteen years and many twists and turns in the path, the first element of ISS will be launched from Russia within the next few months. More than forty launches and nearly five years later, the 950,000 pound station will be complete.

The partners in this gigantic effort include the United States, Russia, Japan, Canada, and more than a dozen countries making up the European Space Agency. Never have so many countries cooperated in a joint effort that is sure to have a monumental effect on all of humanity over the next several decades. In the micro gravity environment of the station many unique types of experimentation can take place that are not possible elsewhere, and a "jumping off place" for future space travel will be provided. The long term scientific benefits of this project to the human race will most certainly exceed our greatest expectations.

The International Space Station will travel in an orbit varying from 160 miles to 260 miles above the earth. At a speed of approximately 17,500 miles per hour, each orbit will require only about one and one half hours to complete. During each orbit the space station will be visible from nearly eighty five percent of the earth's surface, occupied by ninety five percent of the earth's population.

A crew of three will occupy the space station after the third flight, expanding to a total of seven permanent crew members late in the construction phase. The crew members will come from several countries, with the makeup of the crew at any particular time being decided by mutual agreement of the partners.

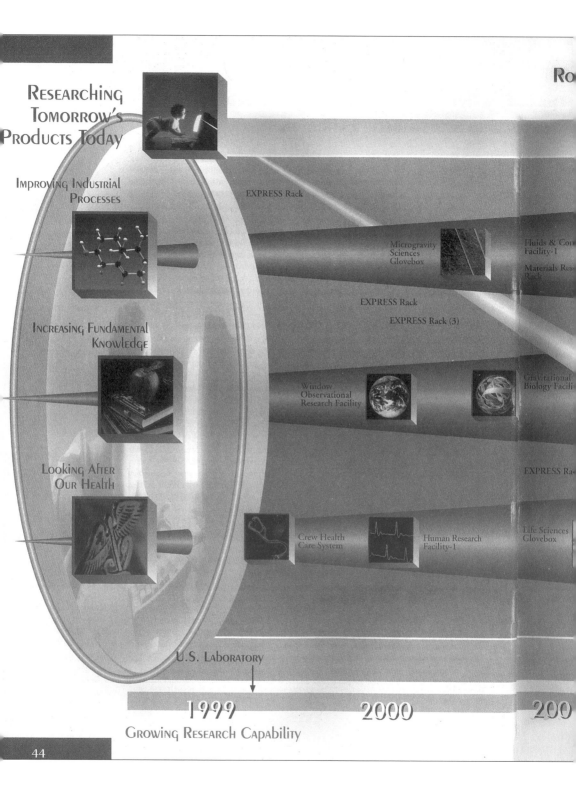

Ro

RESEARCHING
TOMORROW'S
PRODUCTS TODAY

IMPROVING INDUSTRIAL
PROCESSES

EXPRESS Rack

Microgravity
Sciences
Glovebox

Fluids & Cor
Facility-1

Materials Rese
Rack

EXPRESS Rack

EXPRESS Rack (3)

INCREASING FUNDAMENTAL
KNOWLEDGE

Window
Observational
Research Facility

Gravitational
Biology Facili

LOOKING AFTER
OUR HEALTH

EXPRESS Ra

Crew Health
Care System

Human Research
Facility-1

Life Sciences
Glovebox

U.S. LABORATORY

1999   2000   200

GROWING RESEARCH CAPABILITY

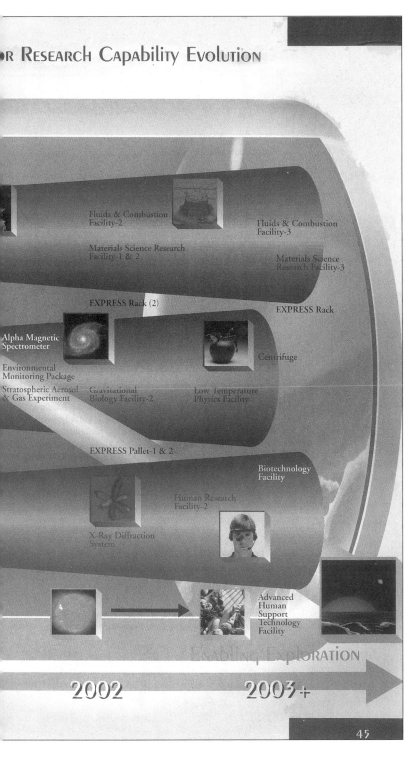

R Research Capability Evolution

Fluids & Combustion Facility-2

Fluids & Combustion Facility-3

Materials Science Research Facility-1 & 2

Materials Science Research Facility-3

EXPRESS Rack (2)

EXPRESS Rack

Alpha Magnetic Spectrometer

Environmental Monitoring Package

Centrifuge

Stratospheric Aerosol & Gas Experiment

Gravitational Biology Facility-2

Low Temperature Physics Facility

EXPRESS Pallet-1 & 2

Biotechnology Facility

Human Research Facility-2

X-Ray Diffraction System

Advanced Human Support Technology Facility

Enabling Exploration

2002

2003+

45

RESEARCH CAPABILITY. The research shown in this photograph is what will take place on the International Space Station. These operations will occur over a number of years. The laboratory itself was placed into orbit in 1999 with additional experimental facilities that will be attached in subsequent years. NASA and the ISS partners maintain an evolving facility deployment and assembly schedule. This sequence may change as the ISS program and station payloads mature. (Photo courtesy of NASA and Wallops Flight Facility.)

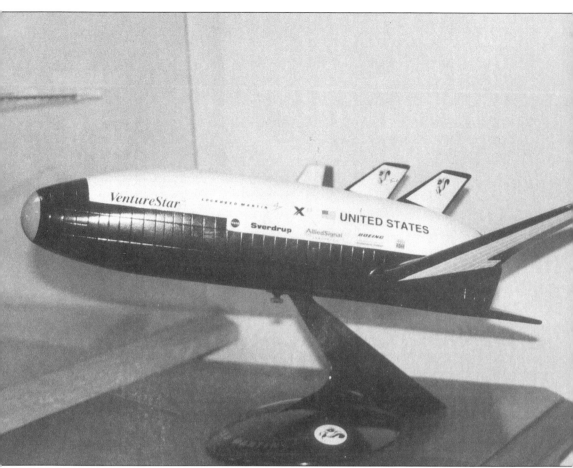

VENTURE STAR. The *Venture Star*, otherwise known as the X-33, is designed to pave the way to a full-scale commercially developed reusable launch vehicle. It is designed as a successor to the space shuttle. The X-33 can take off vertically like a rocket, reaching an altitude of up to 60 miles and lands horizontally like an airplane. It will perform orbital missions and delivery of cargo. The X-33 is unpiloted during missions that don't require an astronaut—launching satellites into orbit, loading equipment, or carrying space station supplies. Wallops Island is being considered as the new home for this project because of its location and fine facilities. (Photo by Bo Bennett.)

Top - 2001	Next	
Atlantis	01-18-01	ISS-5A US Destiny Laboratory Module
Discovery	02-15-01	ISS-5A.1 Destiny Lab outfitting, Leonardo MPLM, crew
Endeavour	04-19-01	ISS-6A Raffaello MPLM, UHF, SSRMS
Columbia	TBD	SpaceHab DM, Triana, MEIDEX
Atlantis	05-17-01	ISS-7A Airlock, HPGS
Discovery	06-21-01	ISS-7A.1 Donatello MPLM, crew
Endeavour	08-23-01	ISS-UF1 MPLM, PV Module batteries
Columbia	09-20-01	Hubble Servicing Mission 3B
Atlantis	10-04-01	ISS-8A ITS S0 Center Truss, Mobile Transporter, crew
Columbia	11-01-01	Research Mission, SpaceHab Double Cargo Module
Top - 2002 - Next		
Endeavour	01-17-02	ISS-UF2 MPLM, MBS
Atlantis	02-14-02	ISS-9A ITS S1 (Right-side truss), CETA, S-Band
Columbia	03-21-02	X-38 Flight Demo
Endeavour	05-16-02	ISS-11A ITS P1 (Left-side truss), CETA
Atlantis	06-13-02	ISS-9A.1 SPP with 4 Solar Arrays
Endeavour	SEPT-TBD	ISS-12A ITS P3/P4 (Left-side truss), PV Module
Discovery	OCT-TBD	ISS-12A.1 ITS P5 (Left-side truss), MPLM

SHUTTLE LAUNCHES. The above lists are future dates for shuttle launches and their missions. The shuttles are based at Kennedy Space Center. At one time the shuttles would land at the Edwards Air Force Base, but they found it was more cost efficient to base the shuttle in Florida. The shuttles are stored in a building that is so large it creates its own weather. (Photo courtesy of NASA and Wallops Flight Facility.)

Top - 2003 - Next		
Atlantis	JAN-TBD	ISS-13A ITS S3/S4 (Right-side truss), PV Module
Columbia	TBD	Reimbursable Mission
Discovery	FEB-TBD	ISS-10A Node 2, Nitrogen Tank
Atlantis	MAY-TBD	ISS-10A.1 US Propulsion Module
Columbia	TBD	Reimbursable Mission
Endeavour	JUNE-TBD	ISS-1J/A JEM ELM PS, SPP
Discovery	SEPT-TBD	ISS-1J Kibo Japanese Experiment Module, JEM RMS
Endeavour	OCT-TBD	ISS-UF3 MPLM, Express Pallet
Columbia	TBD	Hubble telescope servicing flight 4
Top - 2004 - Next		
Discovery	JAN-TBD	ISS-UF4 Express Pallet, SPDM, AMS
Endeavour	FEB-TBD	ISS-2J/A JEM EF, 4 Solar Array Batteries
Columbia	TBD	Reimbursable Mission
Discovery	MAY-TBD	ISS-14A Cupola, 4 SPP Arrays, MMOD
Endeavour	JUNE-TBD	ISS-UF5 MPLM, Express Pallet
Columbia	TBD	Reimbursable Mission
Atlantis	SEPT-TBD	ISS-20A Node 3
Discovery	OCT-TBD	ISS-1E Columbus Attached Pressurized Module (APM)
2005		
Endeavour	JAN-TBD	ISS-17A MPLM, Destiny lab racks
Atlantis	FEB-TBD	ISS-18A US Crew Return Vehicle (CRV)
Discovery	MAR-TBD	ISS-19A MPLM
Endeavour	MAY-TBD	ISS-15A Photovoltaic Module S6
Atlantis	JUNE-TBD	ISS-UF7 Centrifuge Accomodations Module (CAM)
Discovery	JULY-TBD	ISS-UF6 MPLM, batteries
Endeavour	SEPT-TBD	ISS-16A US Habitation module

BIBLIOGRAPHY

Badger, Curtis et.al. *The Barrier Islands: A Photographic History of Life n Hogg, Cobb, Smith, Cedar, Parramore, Metompkin & Assateague*. Harrisburg, PA: Stackpole Books, 1989.

Barnes, Brooks, Miles, Truitt, Barry R. *Seashore Chronicles: Three Centuries of the Virginia Barrier Islands*. N.p.: Virginia University Press, 1997.

Whitelaw, Ralph T. *Virginia's Eastern Shore*. Richmond, VA: Virginia Historical Society, 1951.

Interviews were conducted with the following:

Clark, Jack; Daffin, Phillip; Duffy, Robert; Eastern Shore of Virginia Historical Society; Flowers, Betty; Hall, John; Hines, Lynn Krieger; Howard, Orland; Jacobs, Bob; Jenkins, Richard E.; Jester, Jill; Kohler, Keith; Krieger, Jack; Krieger, Karen; Kulley, Dave; Lappin, Bobby; McCready, Timmy; McIntyre, Vernon; Ogle, Mark, Lt. Commander; Rajala, Dennis; Rodgers, Ronnie; Spinak, Ruth; Taylor, Emmett; and Wallop, Janice.

Other Sources:

Krieger, Richard L., *John Wallops Papers*

NASA, *Improving Life on Earth and In Space, The Nasa Research Plan, An Overview*

Materials from the Educational Center at the Wallops Flight Facility Visitor's Center

Wallops Island Papers

www.nasa.gov

www.navy.mil

www.space.com

www.nsroc.com

www.grdl.noaa.gov

www.fas.org

lisar.larc.nasa.gov

www.rumfart.dk

www.redstone.army.mil

www.thespaceplace